Praise for 30

I remember reading 1 Samuel for the first time many years ago and being fascinated by the stories of Samuel, Saul, and David. What Josh Wredberg has done in this devotional is show us more than just the moralistic lessons we are used to hearing. We see how God has been paving the way for a King and a kingdom. I highly recommend this book for everyone!

—Dr. Matt Carter
Pastor of Preaching & Vision,
The Austin Stone Community Church, Austin, TX
Author, *The Real Win: Pursuing God's Plan for Authentic Success* and
Steal Away Home

The stories in 1 Samuel are fun to read, but God placed them in Scripture for a much greater reason. Josh Wredberg brings us behind the accounts to see and savor the bigger redemptive purposes of God as shown in the life of David and coming King Jesus from his line. Read these devotions to learn about these purposes, but even more, read these devotions to grow in your love for and appreciation of the great God who gave us 1 Samuel.

—Dr. Jon Pratt
Vice President of Academics and Professor of New Testament,
Central Baptist Theological Seminary, Plymouth, MN

With gracious pastoral care and careful biblical accuracy, Josh Wredberg takes us on a journey from heartache in the temple and unforeseen royalty in the pasture, to the majesty of the never-ending kingdom. *30 Days to 1 Samuel* will not only capture your attention, but more importantly, it will kindle your affections for the Truer King, Jesus Christ. Do not just sit back as you read. Instead, lean forward in eager anticipation of God moving your heart to bow before His throne.

—Dan Loggans
Pastor for Preaching and Vision,
Christ Fellowship Church, Sun Prairie, WI

A beautiful picture is sometimes best viewed against a dark background. In the great story of the Bible, few backgrounds are darker, yet more important, than the historical narrative of 1 Samuel. Against this tragic background we learn of three men: Samuel, Saul, and David. Their stories help advance the great story of the Bible; the redemptive story of God's Son who left the glories of heaven to be our substitute and thereby secure our salvation. In Christ we are made righteous before our holy God. I cannot recommend Josh Wredberg's devotional treatment of 1 Samuel highly enough. Read it for your own edification. Read it to be reminded of God's sovereign work in providing for us a king who will one day make all things right. Read it to grow spiritually. You will be blessed!

—Dr. Dave Jaspers
Elder, Ridgewood Baptist Church, Joliet, IL

For those who are not quite sure what to do with the stories of the Old Testament, Josh Wredberg's devotional commentary offers much-needed help. Wredberg helps us understand and apply the book of 1 Samuel in light of the gospel. Far more than a collection of moral lessons drawn from King David's life, 1 Samuel bears witness to David's greater son, Jesus, the King God's people have always needed.

—Dr. David Burnette
Editor at *Radical*, The Resource Ministry of David Platt

In his *30 Days to 1 Samuel* devotional commentary, Dr. Josh Wredberg blends the practical wisdom of a pastor-teacher with the insights of a skillful, biblical scholar. Furthermore, each of his theologically-rich daily studies provides a balance of wonderful humor that keeps readers engaged, illustrations that we can all relate with, and suggestions for 'real life' application. This is an ideal devotional for an individual or the whole family. But most importantly, after 30 days, I believe you will have a clearer picture of Jesus Christ and find yourself in a closer walk with him.

—Dr. David Burggraff
Executive Pastor, Colonial Baptist Church, Cary, North Carolina
Professor of Theology, Shepherds Theological Seminary

Josh is a good friend and careful exegete. His challenging insights on 1 Samuel give the reader a helpful understanding of God's Word so that they can apply it to their life in a meaningful and helpful way. I recommend this book and a chapter a day approach. At the end, you will be greatly encouraged!

—Dr. Clay Burgess
Pastor and Lead Communicator,
Connect Church, Fuquay-Varina, NC

It is a rare teacher of the word who can accurately draw timeless lessons from an Old Testament history book like 1 Samuel and deliver them faithfully across three millennia of cultural, linguistic, economic, and social differences to 21st century people. Josh Wredberg does that in this marvelous devotional commentary, *30 Days to 1 Samuel*. As you read his entries day by day, you will be drawn in by lucid illustrations, instructed by accurate exegesis, and counseled by practical applications. I commend it to you wholeheartedly.

—Dr. Andrew Davis
Senior Pastor, First Baptist Church, Durham, NC
Author, *Revitalize: Biblical Keys to Helping Your Church Come Alive Again* and *An Infinite Journey: Growing Toward Christlikeness*

As I was working my way through this devotional commentary, the essence of the word 'devotion' became what was most prominent. I was confronted with my own weakness and sin as the characters in 1 Samuel came to life, yet at the same time, I was reminded of God's sustaining faithfulness. *30 Days to 1 Samuel* combines clear understanding of the text of 1 Samuel with the same care toward helpful application. Any and all who pick up this devotion will be confronted with the redemptive theme of Christ and moved towards an increased faith in a perfectly faithful God.

—Zach Nelson
Executive Director, The Pillar Network

30 DAYS TO
1 SAMUEL

30 Days to
1 Samuel

Josh Wredberg

Seed Publishing Group, LLC
Timmonsville, South Carolina

30 Days to 1 Samuel: A Devotional Commentary

Published by:
Seed Publishing Group
2570 Double C Farm Ln
Timmonsville, SC 29161
seed–publishing–group.com

Edited by:
Bill Curtis, Ph.D.
Dwayne Milioni, Ph.D.

To order additional copies of this resource visit
www.seed–publishing–group.com.

Library of Congress Control Number: 2019933159

ISBN–13: 978-0-9985451-4-1

Printed in the United States of America

Dedication

To my sons, Jack, Max, and Caed.
May you, like Samuel, listen to the voice of
the Lord and serve him with your whole heart.

Contents

Contents

Foreword

I didn't plan to spend a large chunk of my ministry in theological education. In fact, when I went to seminary, I swore that I would never do doctoral work and I would never teach. What changed my mind? Well, during my first pastorate, I became very disillusioned through a series of interactions with some seasoned pastors. These were men who, by all the standards we measure success in Christian leadership today, were considered to be successful. They pastored large, growing churches. They held denominational positions. The could preach. But as I got to know them beyond their public ministries, I discovered a disconnect between their public lives and their private lives. And as a young pastor in his mid-20s, I didn't know what to do with that irony. I was so discouraged and disappointed that I came close to walking away from ministry leadership.

God in his grace, however, redeemed my crisis. He let me discover something that's haunted me my entire adult life. I came to the realization that we can live out our entire Christian lives in such a way that people will consider us to be successful, and yet all the time be doing it in the flesh. We can be good enough leaders, good enough administrators, good enough communicators, good enough spouses, good enough parents, and good enough employees that people will label us as successful. Yet, we can do every one of these things in our own strength and power, devoid of any dependence upon God. We can be successful in the flesh, yet bankrupt in the spirit. Through that crisis, God burdened me to want to have that conversation with young Christian leaders. That's how I ended up in theological education.

First Samuel is about that same crisis—the crisis of individuals and nations relying upon themselves instead of upon God and His salvation. After seasons of seeming success, Eli and his sons failed as priests, Saul failed as a king, and the nation of Israel failed as a monarchy. They were all relying upon themselves and not upon God. Ronald Youngblood got it right when he said of Israel,

> "Their sin consisted in the fact that they were asking for a king "to lead us and to go out before us and to fight our battles (v. 20)." In other words, they refused to believe that the Lord would grant them victory in his own time and according to his own good pleasure (cf. 2 Sam 8:6, 14). They were willing to exchange humble faith in the protection and power of "The Lord Almighty (1 Sam 1:3)" for misguided reliance on the naked strength of "the fighting men of Israel (2 Sam 24:4)." (Youngblood, 1, 2 Samuel, Expositor's Bible Commentary, 558).

While 1 Samuel closes with the apparent success of David as an up-and-coming leader, it's only a matter of time before even he crashes and burns as a husband and father. While all of these characters demonstrated success on the surface, failure lurked in the shadows when they turned their eyes upon themselves and relied upon their own strength.

My brother, Josh Wredberg, shows us that the Holy Spirit inspired 1 Samuel, at least in part, to show us this vanity and point us to his great salvation on our behalf. In this rich devotional and expositional journey, he takes us on a path that reveals the utter futility of people, nations, and even churches relying upon themselves for success. In contrast, he uncovers numerous diamonds in the rough of life's failures, jewels that hold the secrets to spiritual success that comes only through 1 Samuel's ultimate goal—faith in Jesus Christ. In these pages, you will be encouraged and challenged through the discovery of these spiritual riches. Foremost among them is this profound truth: Delighting in Jesus, experiencing a love relationship with Him, obeying His will, and unreservedly depending upon His grace is our only hope of true success.

—Jim Shaddix, Ph.D., D.Min.
W. A. Criswell Professor of Expository Preaching
Director, Center for Preaching and Pastoral Leadership,
Southeastern Baptist Theological Seminary,
Wake Forest, NC

Preface

When I was in high school, my best friend and I played basketball all the time. We would shoot hoops in his driveway for hours, we played on the same team at school, and we watched games on television. Almost every day we played basketball. One night we went to the video store looking for a movie to watch and were thrilled when we found one with the word *basketball* in the title. We watched the entire plotless, pointless movie, and there was only one basketball scene. I do not know if you have ever had an experience where you picked something because of the title and realized the title really did not capture the content.

If you are unfamiliar with 1 and 2 Samuel, you may be surprised by the content. The previous three books of the Bible are Joshua, Judges, and Ruth. The main character in the book of Joshua is Joshua, the main characters in the book of Judges are the Judges, and the main character in the book of Ruth is Ruth. When you finish Ruth and turn to 1 Samuel, you are prepared for a book primarily about Samuel, and when the book begins, Samuel is the main character. But after the first quarter of the book, the focus changes.

Preface

The main character in 1 and 2 Samuel is not Samuel, the main character is David. And we discover as the Bible continues that the ultimate focus of the book is not David, but a coming king from the line of David. This book, which begins with Samuel and chronicles the rise and reign of King David is part of a much larger story; a story which began in the Garden of Eden with the promise of a conquering king and ends with an eternal kingdom governed by King Jesus.

Over the next thirty days, we will study stories about a king and his kingdom. These stories show us how God's plan to raise up a king to build a kingdom is pictured in David and fulfilled in Jesus. My hope and prayer is that this study in Samuel will provide a clearer picture of Jesus Christ, and that seeing Jesus more clearly will deepen your love for him. And when your love for Jesus grows, you will find listening to him, doing his will, and keeping his commands easier and sweeter.

One more thing . . . this book is part of a larger series of books that is being developed by Seed Publishing Group; it is called *30 Days to the Bible*. Each year, several new books will be added to this series until all of the books of the Bible have been covered. Renowned scholars and pastors from around the country will be writing books for this exciting, new series. So, if you like *30 Days to 1 Samuel*, pick up one of the other *30 Days* books, and keep your eyes open for new books in the series.

Finally, Seed Publishing Group is an independent publisher committed to bringing great resources to both individual Christians and the local church (please visit them at www.seed-publishing-group.com). As part of that commitment, they are partners with The Pillar Network for church planting (www.thepillarnetwork.com). $1 from each sale of *30 Days to 1 Samuel* goes directly to church plants throughout North America. Thank you for purchasing *30 Days to 1 Samuel,* and thank you for investing in church planting.

Desperate Times

1 Samuel 1:1–16

When life falls apart, most children turn to their mom. A young child falls and skins his knee, and without a moment's hesitation screams, "Mommy!" Where do desperate adults turn? When life falls apart due to bankruptcy, cancer, miscarriage, unemployment, or divorce, where do we turn for help? The popular modern stories—like Superman, Batman, and Star Wars—turn to an outside source of help in the most desperate times. These stories acknowledge something we all know deep down, something God has wired into our DNA. When everything is bleak and the hour is dark, we need supernatural help. When we are desperate, we need help greater than any human can provide. These stories echo the true story of our world, written for us in the Bible. What we find in story after story is that God delivers desperate people. 1 Samuel opens with a small story that reinforces this theme.

The desperate person was a woman named Hannah, and she was desperate because she was childless (v. 2). We know that her barrenness was her issue, not her husbands, because her husband took a second wife and bore children with her. Hannah had no children, while his other wife,

> *Hannah, in her desperation, did not turn to an idol. Instead she cried out to God in her desperation.*

Peninnah, had multiple children. This deepened Hannah's despair (v. 6). Since infertility was seen as a curse, she was ridiculed by Peninnah and likely by others around her. People would have openly questioned what Hannah did wrong. They would have sneered, "She must have done something terrible for God to make her barren."

Hannah's desperation was especially severe on the yearly, family trip to Shiloh to offer sacrifices. Peninnah would have received multiple portions—one for her and one for each of her children. When those portions were handed out, Hannah was presented with a visible reminder that she had no kids. In her despair, she lost her appetite, and her husband asked her why she was crying (v. 8). Then followed it up with an insensitive question: "Am I not better than ten sons?" The barrenness, ridicule, and loneliness all combined to produce incredible pain, which left Hannah "deeply distressed (v. 10)." This background information helps us better understand the depth of her pain. She was at her low point—broken and hopeless.

Where did Hannah turn in her desperation? I was talking with my 9-year old son about this story one day, and I was trying to remind him of what happened. I mentioned Hannah and tried to prompt his memory by saying, "She couldn't have a baby, so she..." And without a moment's hesitation he said, "She stole one!" (Who are this kid's Sunday School teachers?) Hannah did not steal a baby, though there is an account in Scripture of a desperate woman stealing another woman's child. Desperate people often do desperate things.

Hannah could have done what many other women in that culture did. Hannah lived during the time of the Judges, and when you read through the book of Judges you see two names repeated: Baal and Asherah. While Baal was a more common term to describe a false god (likely the god who it was believed could control the weather), Asherah was a Canaanite goddess of fertility. Many of the Israelite families had a Asherah pole on their land or in their community where they would go and offer sacrifices to this pagan goddess hoping for a child. Hannah, in her desperation, did not turn to an idol. Instead she cried out to God in her desperation. Four times in this passage, the text says Hannah prayed (vv. 10, 12, 13, 16). In her desperation, she cried out to God for help.

Hannah's prayer was humble. She knew who God was, and she knew who she was. She addressed God as the "Lord of Armies"—the first time we find this description in the Bible. She understood God's power—he controls heavenly armies—and she was under no illusion about her own power. She was just a "servant (v. 11)." She, in her weakness, could not conceive a child, but she knew God had the power to do it. If he controlled heavenly armies, then he could open her womb.

Why do we struggle to pray? It could be we doubt God's power, but it is more likely we overestimate our own. We are too self-confident. Only when we feel powerless, do we turn to God in prayer. Our problem is not that we move from powerlessness to power, but rather we move from feeling our powerlessness to ignoring it. Hannah knew she was desper-

Hannah did not offer generic prayers, but she poured out her heart to the God she knew; the God whose covenant love had led her people out of bondage and into a new land.

Effective prayer is honest prayer.

ate—she understood her weakness, so she turned to the God of powerful armies and asked Him to do something she could not accomplish on her own.

Hannah's prayer was not only humble, but it was also personal. She knew God, and she was honest about what she felt. Throughout this chapter, Hannah uses God's covenant name (Yahweh). Every time you see the word LORD in all lowercase letters, it is a translation of the name Yahweh. Hannah did not offer generic prayers, but she poured out her heart to the God she knew; the God whose covenant love had led her people out of bondage and into a new land.

She knew her God, and she was honest with him. She did not sanitize her feelings, but brought all of the raw pain and frustration before God. She brought God her "great anxiety and vexation (v. 16)." The word "vexation" can be translated "resentment." Do you ever feel like you have to get your life cleaned up before you can pray? You realize you have sinned, you have ignored God, you have chased after your own will, and you think, "I really messed up today, I cannot pray. I cannot tell God what I really think."God knows you better than you know yourself. He knows your sin and guilt, your weakness and fear, your frustration and despair. Effective prayer is honest prayer. It is being honest with God about your struggles. If you feel resentment, do not try to work it out on your own in order to pray. Pray in order to work it out with God's help.

Hannah's prayer was humble, personal, and scriptural. She asked God to "look on the affliction of your servant (v. 11)." The Hebrew words for "look" and "affliction" are found together in some earlier accounts in Scripture.

When Moses stood before God at the burning bush, God commanded him to go to Egypt to rescue his people. Why? "Because," God said, "I have surely *seen* the *affliction* of my people (Ex 3:7)." Though translated differently, those are the same words Hannah used in her prayer. When the enslaved nation of Israel heard from Aaron about God's promise to deliver them from slavery, "The people believed; and when they heard that the Lord had visited the people of Israel and that he had *seen* their *affliction*, they bowed their heads and worshiped (Ex 4:31)." Hannah's reflection on Scripture informed her understanding of who God was and what he could do. She knew he was a God powerful enough to deliver her from her affliction, and she knew he was a God loving enough to listen to her plea. Meditating on Scripture informs our praying. It gives us faith that God will listen and act. That is why prayer and Scripture reading are the breathing and heartbeat of spiritual life.

Hannah knew where to turn in her desperation. Her praying is described as "pouring out her soul (v. 15)." Where do you turn when your soul is overwhelmed? Hannah knew she could turn to God and pour her soul out to him. She went to God and asked him to open her womb, even though he was the one who had closed it (v. 5). God's sovereignty should not lead us to passivity but to prayer. We pray to the God who is in control of all things. We pray to the God high enough to control angelic armies, yet close enough to listen to us even when we do not know what to say. Desperate times do not call for desperate measures, but for prayer to the God who delivers desperate people.

> *She knew he was a God powerful enough to deliver her from her affliction, and she knew he was a God loving enough to listen to her plea.*

Food for Thought When something difficult happens, what is your first response? Think about the most recent time you received unexpected or unwanted news. It could be a bill that was twice the normal amount, or a routine doctor's visit that was anything but routine. When the news came, who did you call? Did you call a parent or child? A family member or friend? How many people did you turn to for help and comfort before you turned to God?

Make a plan to work through this book over the next thirty days. Find a time each day when you will read it and record your **Faith in Action** thoughts. If you do not normally journal, consider keeping one while you do this study. You do not have to write an essay each day, but jot down a thought or two to meditate on throughout the day. You will be surprised how much writing something down, even just a sentence, can help you apply the truths from God's Word to your life. If you have never studied a book of the Bible with someone, consider giving them a copy and meeting weekly to discuss what you are learning.

Prayer Praise God that he is a personal God who listens to the desperate pleas of his people. Ask God to help you understand your own powerlessness to fix your deepest problems. Pray that you will see clearly your own inability and turn from attempts to rescue yourself. End your time of prayer by recalling moments God has delivered you and thanking him for his deliverance.

God Delivers

1 Samuel 1:17–28

When Hannah arrived at the tabernacle in Shiloh to pray, she was not alone. Sitting in a corner of the tabernacle was Eli, the priest. When he first saw Hannah, he thought she was drunk. His response tells us something about both the spiritual climate in Israel and Eli's discernment. She assured him she was not drunk, but heartbroken over her barrenness. Eli responded, "Go in peace, and the God of Israel grant your petition that you have made to him (v. 17)." Whether Eli's words should be taken as a promise or not, Hannah saw God's care in them, and she headed back to her family knowing God had heard her prayer.

In the New Testament, we find a command given to Christians to cast all our anxieties on Christ because he cares for us (1 Pet 5:7). Sometimes we wonder what that looks like. How do I cast my anxieties on Jesus? Hannah is a real-life example. She walked into that place of worship with a burden on her back that was about to crush her. Through great spiritual struggle, she took that burden, shrugged it off, and left it in God's hands. When she walked out, she did so unencumbered—the burden had been cast on the one who cared for her. What she did in that temple

> *God heard her prayer and then acted towards her in a very personal, gracious way.*

was act in faith. She not only cried out to God, but she trusted God to answer. What burden is crushing you right now? Perhaps it is a child who resists the gospel. Every day you wake up with this burden that drags you down, threatening to crush you. By the middle of the day, you are about ready to give up—you just cannot carry that weight any longer. Jesus invites you to hand that burden to Him. Maybe it is not a wayward child, but a demanding job, a dying parent, a terminal disease, a constant temptation, or a spiritual defeat. Cry out to God, and trust him to deliver you from that burden.

After Hannah and her family returned home, "the Lord remembered her (v. 19)." God never forgets, but the author of 1 Samuel uses this phrase to show that God heard her prayer and then acted towards her in a very personal, gracious way. God listened to her plea, and he responded tenderly and personally to her need. He caused her to conceive, providing her with the son for which she had prayed.. Her shame had been removed by the sovereign grace of God.

Hannah made a commitment to God that if she had a son, he would live under a Nazarite vow, never cutting his hair or drinking wine, and he would serve in the temple. In other words, he would be fully devoted to God. This vow is a picture of complete devotion, withholding nothing. But it was not just her son, Samuel, who would be completely devoted to God. Consider what Hannah was doing. She was giving her only child away to serve God. She was giving her prize to God. This son God had given her, was going to be given back to him. She would offer God the thing most precious to her. What is most precious to you? Have you given it to God? It was on January 8, 1956 that Jim Elliot died at the hands of the Auca tribe in Ecuador. He famously said, "He is no fool who gives what he cannot keep to gain what he cannot lose." But he did not just say it, he lived it. He gave the life which he could not keep in order to gain that which cannot be lost—the glory of Jesus among a people who had never heard. When I think of someone who offered God full devotion—everything—I think of Jim Elliot. But I also think of my friends, Steve and Kristi, living in East Asia, who have given up a comfortable life in the United States to reach Muslims with the gospel. I think of those who sit in my church each week who have given up time, money, position, and ego in order to advance the kingdom of God in our community. The only fitting response to God's deliverance is to offer him our devotion.

When Samuel was three years old, Hannah loaded him up and took a trip to Shiloh. She brought Samuel to Eli and said, "'For this child I prayed, and the LORD has granted me my petition that I made to him. Therefore I have lent him to the LORD. As long as he lives, he is lent to the LORD.' And he worshiped the LORD there (vv. 27-28)." Imagine the emotion of that moment. Hannah was about to leave her only child at the temple to permanently serve God there. As she walked with him holding his hand, she knew she would come back alone and empty-handed. How could she give God the most precious thing in her life? God's deliverance produced Hannah's devotion. She had experienced God's grace at her very lowest moment, and it was his grace which led to the gift of her son. Her act of devotion is a living illustration

He is no fool who gives what he cannot keep to gain what he cannot lose.

The only fitting response to God's deliverance is to offer him our devotion.

of what the apostle Paul wrote to the Romans: "I appeal to you therefore, brothers, by the mercies of God, to present your bodies as a living sacrifice, holy and acceptable to God, which is your spiritual worship (Rom 12:1)."Look at the mercies of God. See how wonderful they are. Ponder his grace to you. Now give yourself to him, and do what pleases him—not to earn, not to repay, but to worship. In gratitude for his grace, give him each day as a gift.

This is what faith looks like. Faith begins with an honest assessment of our own inability. We are unable to provide what we need—we cannot save ourselves, we cannot secure our own future, we need help. But who can help us? God can. But will he help us? Yes, because he is gracious. We respond to his grace with faith—trusting him to do what he promised. When he does, then we serve him out of joy and gratitude. We offer him everything we have and everything we are because we know he who delivered us from sin and death will provide and protect us all our days.

This story of Hannah and Samuel is located in this spot for multiple reasons. One is to give us an example of what faith looks like, especially during a dark time in Israel's history. Hannah shows us what it looks like to trust God for deliverance when everything is dark and scary. But that is not the only reason it is here. If it were, we might misinterpret it. We might view it as an ironclad promise to all infertile women that God will give them a baby. There were certainly other faith-filled, barren women in Israel at that time who never did conceive. Many of us know women like that in our lives. This story is here to point us to something bigger than Hannah and Samuel. What happens on an individual level for Hannah has both national and global ramifications. Hannah is the nation of Israel, and ultimately, the world in microcosm. She was desperate and could not solve her problem, so she cried out to God. He delivered her through a son born in a supernatural way. The birth of this son instituted a new age in Israel. Israel will move from a collection of tribes to a unified country under the leadership of a king. More importantly, a kingly line will be established which leads to the birth of King Jesus. The story of Hannah reveals the intention of God to deliver his people, and that deliverance will come when the promised Son is born. Like Hannah, we are hopeless, afflicted and broken-hearted, though unlike Hannah our affliction is due to our own sin. Just as Hannah turned to God for help, our only hope is to cry out to God for deliverance. God's deliverance comes in the form of a Son, born in a supernatural way, zealous for the temple, who is anointed as King forever. Faith in this Son leads to deliverance and should produce a life of devotion and worship.

I recently finished reading a book on the civil war and was reminded of the number of wounded and dead after the major battles. Often in the aftermath of a battle, a flag of truce would be flown, and soldiers could safely re-enter the battlefield to collect the wounded and take them back to their camp for medical treatment. After one particularly vicious battle, the generals on either side disputed the terms of the truce, and so neither side could safely enter the battlefield to collect the wounded. For two days, the wounded lay in the field, crying out for help. Lying in their own blood, many with

God's deliverance produced Hannah's devotion.

If you are wounded by sin or broken by despair, call out to God for help. He will deliver you.

mangled limbs, they cried out for someone to come and save them. Soldiers from both sides could hear the cries and screams, but could do nothing about it. By the time the truce was agreed upon, all but one wounded soldier had died.

When you cry out to God for help, he will never sit on the sideline and watch you suffer. He will always respond. If you are wounded by sin or broken by despair, call out to God for help. He will deliver you. Everyone and everything else are like those soldiers hunkered down behind the lines, powerless to save you. God is not. He hears, he remembers, and he acts in grace.

Are there any burdens crushing you right now? Have you cast those burdens on Jesus who cares for you? One way to cast those burdens on Jesus is to identify them by name, and begin praying regularly for Jesus to either remove them or strengthen you to bear them. After identifying the burden, ask a friend to help you locate promises in Scripture which remind you of Jesus' grace. Write those promises down and review them when the burden threatens to overwhelm you.

Hannah dedicated Samuel to the Lord's use. Nothing was more precious to her than Samuel. What is most precious to you? Make a list of the five things most precious to you, whether people, activities, or tasks. Evaluate each one, asking, "Have I given this to God?" If you have not, consider what steps you need to take to dedicate it wholly to his service.

Prayer

Thank God for the mercy he has shown you through Jesus Christ, then offer your life to him as a living sacrifice. Look at today's schedule and pray for each event, dedicating it to the Lord's use. Ask God for wisdom to serve him in every activity and conversation.

Shout for Joy

1 Samuel 2:1–10

We sat in the living room, knowing there was no hope. With only 25 seconds left and no time outs, our favorite football team could not make it into field goal range. The one point deficit may have well been one hundred. But a miracle happened. We completed a pass, the defender missed the tackle, and the wide receiver crossed the goal line with no time remaining. We won. When it became clear that we would score, people in my house started screaming and running around. We went crazy. This unexpected reversal of fortune caused us to shout for joy.

Today's passage records Hannah's shout for joy. She, too, had an unexpected reversal of fortune. No longer barren, she had given birth to a son. She turned her face to heaven and said, "My heart rejoices..." She was overwhelmed by joy and could not keep silent. Her song of joy came because she had a son, but it celebrates truths deeper than his birth. Having a child is a great reason to shout for joy, but Hannah reveals some greater reasons to rejoice. In Hannah's prayer, we find five reasons she shouted for joy. Every follower of Jesus Christ can shout for joy for the very same reasons.

> *Her joy did not flow out of her circumstances, but out of a right relationship with the Creator.*

First, we can shout for joy because we know the God who is faithful all the time. The center of Hannah's joy was her relationship with the living God. She began her song, "My heart exults *in the Lord* (v. 1). " Her joy did not flow out of her circumstances, but out of a right relationship with the Creator. Her circumstances were not easy; she had "enemies" (v. 1). For years, her enemies taunted her and made her feel unworthy. In her despair, she turned to the Lord and asked him to intervene, and he did. She described his intervention as "your salvation (v. 1). " Hannah was not just responding this way because God had given her a son. She responded this way because God listened to her prayer, lifted her up from despair, and showed himself strong on her behalf. Her joy was not rooted in the birth of Samuel but in the response of God. God heard her and acted in love.

Hannah saw God's faithfulness to her and realized how unique it was. She said, "There is none holy like the LORD: for there is none besides you (v. 2)." No one is like God. His faithfulness to his people far exceeds anyone else's faithfulness. This book of 1 Samuel is a testimony to his faithfulness to his people. They were in a dark season, characterized by faithlessness and rebellion. Yet God did not give up on them. He sent Samuel, who would anoint a king to lead Israel out of the dark ages and into a period of peace and stability.

Second, we can shout for joy because we know the God who judges the arrogant. One of Hannah's dominant themes was God's judgment on those who exalt themselves. She employed a number of images to make this point: the bows of the mighty are broken (v. 4), those who were full hire themselves out for bread (v. 5), the woman with many sons is forlorn (v. 5), and the wicked are cut off in darkness (v. 9). Her first statement is the most significant and is illustrated throughout 1 Samuel. She said, "Talk no more so very proudly (v. 3)." More literally, "Do not continue to say, 'Tall, tall.'" The concept of "tall" plays an important role in the coming events in Israel. The very first king of Israel was a man named Saul. When he was chosen to lead the nation, people were surprised because he was a nobody from a nothing family. But he did have one notable characteristic. He was a head taller than anyone else (9:2). He failed as a king, but the problem was not his height; it was his attitude. God gave him victories early in his reign, and he began to believe he was "tall, tall." He became arrogant, and God brought him low. This same truth is illustrated later in the book when a young shepherd boy stepped up to defend God's honor against a giant. This "tall, tall" giant demeaned the living God, and God judged him. Young David hurled a stone, and the giant fell. He was brought low. God opposes the arrogant. No matter how tall they think they are, God brings them low.

Third, we shout for joy because we know the God who exalts the lowly. God not only humbles the exalted, but he exalts the humble. Look at the vivid imagery Hannah used to make her point: the feeble are clothed with strength (v. 4), those who are starving hunger no more (v. 5), and the woman who is childless gives birth to seven (v. 5). Feeble, starving, barren—can you think of people in more desperate need? God, in his grace and mercy, lifts these desperate people up. This is his grace. He does not exalt them because they are worthy, but be-

No one is like God. His faithfulness to his people far exceeds anyone else's faithfulness.

> We need to believe that God is working in this world as he says he is in his Word, and believing it will change how we see everything.

cause he is compassionate. God exalts the lowly.

His grace is pictured again in verse eight. The "ash heap" is not only the town dump, but also the town sewer. Those who had no place to go and no food to eat, often found themselves at the trash heap looking for scraps to eat and a warm place to sleep. If you lived in the town dump, you were less than a nobody. You were an outcast, a pariah. God reaches down from heaven, takes a hand covered in garbage and sewage, and pulls that person out of the trash. He then brings them to sit with those most respected in the city. And he gives them a "seat of honor." That phrase "seat of honor" is used elsewhere to describe God's own throne (Jer 14:21; 17:12). God does not just give the needy a seat with the nobles. He gives the needy his own seat. What a beautiful picture of the Gospel. Jesus Christ lifts us out of the trash heap of sin and sorrow, and he gives us his own seat. He takes our sin and gives us his righteousness. We are invited into God's home and family and made heirs. This is a reason to shout for joy.

Fourth, we can shout for joy because we know the God who is powerful enough to act. 1 Samuel records a number of battles between Israel and the surrounding nations. When Israel won the battle, it was done in a way that made it clear the victory came from God, not from superior military strength. There is only one God who has this kind of power, and Hannah knew Him (v.6, 9). With eyes of faith, she saw the power of God operating above and beyond human powers. She saw the world as it truly is.

We say, "Seeing is believing," but the Bible says the opposite, "Believing is seeing." We need to believe that

God is working in this world as he says he is in his Word, and believing it will change how we see everything. We serve the God who is powerful enough to act, and it allows us to shout for joy even when things do not go as we have planned.

Fifth, we can shout for joy because we know the God who has sent the perfect king. Hannah located her hope and joy in the promise of a king who would set the world right (v. 10). He will rule in perfection. This is where the book of 1 Samuel and the Bible as a whole leads. It leads to Jesus. Only Jesus is strong enough to shoulder the expectations of the world. Only Jesus is mighty enough to accomplish what we need. Jesus (the Messiah, or anointed one) will one day rule in power and peace.

On January 13, 2018, an alert was sent to cellphones across Hawaii. It read, "BALLISTIC MISSILE THREAT INBOUND TO HAWAII. SEEK IMMEDIATE SHELTER. THIS IS NOT A DRILL." As you can imagine, people were terrified. Emergency sirens went off, and crowds rushed to shelters. It turned out the alert was a mistake. No missile was inbound. But it could happen. We live in a world with ballistic missiles, crazy dictators, corrupt judges, violent terrorists, abusive parents, dishonest bosses, and unfair teachers. People in positions of authority abuse their authority for their own benefit. Will it ever end? Jesus, who came the first time to defeat death and the grave, will come again. He will establish a kingdom without missiles, and dictators, and sickness, and even tears. That is a reason to shout for joy.

Only Jesus is mighty enough to accomplish what we need.

What makes you shout for joy? How about this? You know a faithful, powerful God who humbles the exalted and exalts the humble. And you know his Son, Jesus, who is victorious over sin and death.

Food for Thought God is faithful and unchanging, not moody and capricious like the false gods of the pagan nations surrounding Israel. A lot of the gods of our culture are the same way—gods like health, beauty, success, career, sex, and comfort. Are any of these gods faithful? Can we count on them? Or are we constantly trying to appease them by offering sacrifice after sacrifice? These gods we give our lives to cannot bring lasting joy because their favor is momentary. All of these things we are tempted to live for are fleeting, not faithful. Only God is an unmoving rock.

Faith in Action

Like Saul and Goliath, we can start to view ourselves as tall and exalted. Often it happens when God allows us to see success. In what part of your life are you tempted toward pride? Make a list of everything God has done and has given you to make you successful in that part of your life. Thank him for what he has given you. Gratitude to God for his grace will conquer your temptation to pride.

Prayer

As you pray today, shout for joy to God. It may feel strange to shout to God, but he commands us to (Ps 33:1). Go in a room and shut the door or go for a walk in the woods and loudly thank God for who he is and what he has done for you through Jesus Christ.

Spiritual Blindness

1 Samuel 2:11–3:8

Eli served as priest at the tabernacle in Shiloh. It appears he functioned as Israel's high priest; the spiritual leader of Israel. What was the spiritual condition of God's people under Eli's leadership? God's people were not hearing from God (v. 1). A "vision" was more than an event; it was a message, and the message had gone missing. This description of God's silence and Eli's leadership helps us understand the book of Judges—the heartbreaking account of Israel's repeated failure to obey God. A cycle of disobedience, judgment, repentance, and deliverance propels the storyline of Judges. God's people disobeyed him by worshiping false gods. God judged Israel through the hands of a foreign nation. After a time of slavery, Israel repented and begged God for deliverance. He heard their cries and raised up a judge who delivered them. Without fail, Israel, after having been delivered by God's good hand, fell again into disobedience. When you read through Judges you are struck by the foolishness of God's people. Why did they constantly fall back into the sin which brought devastating consequences?

> *The most dangerous place for a person to be is in a church that does not preach the Bible.*

The answer is clear. God's Word was forgotten. The people were living in a state that the world calls freedom—each man free to do what was right in their own eyes—but the end result was slavery. Whenever the Word of God is forgotten, the result will be disobedience and sin. The Psalmist writes, "How can a young man keep his way pure? By walking according to your word (Ps 119:9)." The reverse is also true: How can a young man keep his way defiled? By ignoring God's word.

Like gold hidden deep in a mineshaft, God's Word was rare in Israel. His revelation was infrequent. Who was to blame? The answer is found in verse two: "At that time Eli, whose eyesight had begun to grow dim so that he could not see, was lying down in his own place." The author of Samuel loves to highlight physical characteristics to make a spiritual point. In yesterday's lesson we saw how he used "tall, tall" as a synonym for pride. Later in the book, when the author highlights someone's incredible height—like Saul or Goliath—he does so to reveal something about their spiritual condition. He tells us they were tall so we will remember what he said earlier about God humbling the "tall, tall." He does this again in chapter three. In verse one, he told us that there was no frequent vision, and in the very next verse he describes Eli as one "whose eyesight had begun to grow dim so that he could not see." He is laying the responsibility at Eli's feet. The reason God's Word was rare was because the spiritual leader of Israel could not see.

Three times God called Samuel before finally appearing to him in verse ten. This three-fold repetition reveals that Eli no longer recognized God's voice. He was not only growing blind, but he had also grown deaf. Only after the third time does Eli perceive it was God who was calling Samuel. What a sad commentary on the priest. He, of all people, should have recognized what was happening, but he had grown insensitive to the things of God.

This happens to professing Christians who are constantly around the things of God without being exposed to the Word of God. The most dangerous place for a person to be is in a church that does not preach the Bible. The constant religious exercise and vague god-talk serves to harden a person to God himself. Weekly religious exercise without the life-giving Word of God is akin to pouring another layer of cement on a person's heart. They grow comfortable with their own version of God: safe, palatable, accepting, and non-judgmental. This happens because they are never actually confronted with the true God of the Bible, a God who is certainly not safe, who judges sin and sinners, and who has promised to pour his wrath out on those who have rejected his Son. Religious exercise without the life-giving Word of God calluses a person's heart to the truth.

Eli's great sin was choosing his sons' acceptance over God's. He knew their sin. He was fully aware of their blasphemous work as priests, yet he chose the wrath of God over the wrath of his sons. His actions with his children reveal a heart that was never submitted to God. Though he rebuked them (2:24) for their sin, he did nothing more. He was not willing to take the necessary steps to restrain them. Ultimately, Eli did what was right in his own eyes, and as a result, he was a failure in God's.

When Samuel pronounced the judgment on Eli, Eli said something which at first seemed

Religious exercise without the life-giving Word of God calluses a person's heart to the truth.

> "
>
> *Morality is no substitute for knowing God.*
>
> "

pious, but upon further reflection revealed his ignorance of God (v. 18). When Samuel made the pronouncement, Eli did not argue. He did not dispute the charges. He did not lie. He did not minimize what had been done. But he also did not ask for mercy. Here was a priest whose job was to meet sinners who came to the temple with their sacrifices. Upon receiving their sacrifices, he would place them on the altar and offer them to God. What was the point of this daily activity? These sinners had come to confess their sin, offer their sacrifice, and receive forgiveness from God. The whole point of the sacrificial system was to reveal God's holiness (he punishes sin) and his mercy (he has made a way for sinners to be forgiven). Yet the spiritual leader of Israel did not get it. He did not understand the God he had been serving his entire life. When he said, "It is the Lord. Let him do what seems good to him (v. 18)," he acknowledged that his sin deserved punishment, but he also acknowledged that he never understood the mercy of God.

If Eli had known God and listened to God's Word, he would have remembered the account of Abraham who begged God to spare wicked Sodom (Gen 18). He would have thought about Moses, who pleaded for God to be merciful to the Israelites when they formed a calf out of gold and worshipped it (Ex 32).But Eli's response leaves no doubt that he did not know God. He knew some things about God. He was busy in religious work, but he did not know God. For if he had known God, he would have known the mercy of God.

In his interaction with Samuel, Eli demonstrated some commendable qualities. He was very kind to Samuel. If you were woken up three times in the middle of the night by a little child, how would you respond? He was humble in his dealings with Samuel. Even though Samuel could be perceived as a threat, Eli helped him, encouraged him, and gave him wise advice when Samuel came to him. Even the judgment on Eli's house was not because of any gross immorality on his part. As far as we know, he did not steal the sacrifice or have sex with the temple servants like his sons. He even responded with sadness and concern over his sons' wickedness. Despite his considerable morality, it was not enough. Morality is no substitute for knowing God.

You may think your morality will give you good standing before God. You may evaluate your life like a balance sheet, and in your opinion the good far outweighs the bad. No matter how many good things you do—even if you served your entire life in God's temple like Eli—the balance sheet will never tip in your favor. One act of disobedience against an infinitely holy God dooms you to eternal punishment. In chapter two, Eli asked the question, "If someone sins against the Lord, who can intercede for him (v. 25)?" The only hope for sinful mankind was that God would provide an interceder, and he did: Jesus. God's own son came to intercede for sinners. He lived a perfect life, died to pay for our sins, and rose again as a sign of God's acceptance. His perfect balance sheet can becomes yours if you turn from your sin and trust him as your Savior. Do not be fooled, morality is no substitute for knowing God.

The only hope for sinful mankind was that God would provide an interceder, and he did: Jesus.

Food for Thought Eli serves as a warning for anyone who is in a position of spiritual leadership. A spiritual position does not guarantee spiritual growth. If it was possible for the acting high priest to be blind to God's Word, then it is certainly possible for the eyesight of pastors, small group leaders, or Sunday school teachers to grow dim. The greater the influence, the more dangerous the temptation to focus on something other than the Word of God. Similarly, it's tragic to discover that Eli's sons weren't even God-fearers, despite the fact that they served as priests. What about you? Have you had a personal encounter with Jesus Christ as your Savior? If you have doubts about that, please take time today to read "Finding L.I.F.E. in Jesus" at the end of this book.

How are you storing God's Word in your heart (Ps 119:11)? Find a good plan for Scripture memorization. Many good ones **Faith in Action** are available online. Pick out some helpful verses, write them on sticky notes, and place them on your bathroom mirror, kitchen window, or car dash so you will see them regularly. Be involved in your local church. Attend Bible studies, small groups, and Sunday worship. Download a sermon podcast from a faithful Bible teacher. You are not lacking for opportunities to store God's Word in your heart.

Prayer Pray for the leaders of your local church. Pray that they will not assume their position protects them from growing dull to the things of God. Pray that they will stay personally committed to the Word of God. If you are part of a faithful church, thank God for the leaders who care for you, and ask God to help you encourage them this week.

Listening to God

1 Samuel 3:9–21

Samuel was dedicated to God's service before he was born and had grown up in the temple under the leadership of Eli. By the first verse of chapter three, we have been told about Samuel's activity in the temple five times: "And the boy ministered to the LORD in the presence of Eli the priest (2:11)," "Samuel was ministering before the LORD, a boy clothed with a linen ephod (2:18)," "And the young man Samuel grew in the presence of the LORD (2:21)," "Now the young man Samuel continued to grow both in stature and in favor with the LORD and also with man (2:26)," and "Now the young man Samuel was ministering to the LORD under Eli (3:1)." A significant shift was taking place in the leadership of Israel, and it happened through this young man. The repetition of "to the Lord", "before the Lord," and "with the Lord" reveals how his leadership would be different from what came before him. Samuel would be a leader who knew the Lord. He would be a leader who listened and submitted to the will and Word of God.

> *Samuel was being exalted because he listened and submitted to the Word of God.*

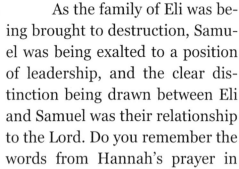

As the family of Eli was being brought to destruction, Samuel was being exalted to a position of leadership, and the clear distinction being drawn between Eli and Samuel was their relationship to the Lord. Do you remember the words from Hannah's prayer in chapter two? She said, "The Lord brings low and he exalts (2:7)." Eli was being brought low because he failed to listen to God, and Samuel was being exalted because he listened and submitted to the Word of God. This contrast moves the story forward. The author even makes a point to contrast where Eli and Samuel slept. Eli was "lying down in his own place (v. 2)." Samuel was "lying down in the temple of the Lord, where the ark of God was (v. 3)." This detail is not included because Eli was sinning, but to vividly demonstrate the trajectory of these two men. Eli, though moral and upstanding, was ultimately about Eli. He was ruled by his own word. He was independent. He lived "in his own house." In contrast, Samuel was in the presence of the Lord. He was busy obeying God. He was ruled by the Word of God. He was consciously dependent on his God.

This account of Samuel's call is instructive because of Samuel's example and his role. His example reveals the proper response to God: God's people respond to God's Word by listening. Four times God called out to Samuel and four times Samuel eagerly responded to the call. The first three times he ran to Eli thinking it was the priest who called. He was awakened in the middle of the night, and he sprinted to the priest. He was a young man eager to listen. After Eli perceived it was the Lord, Samuel responded to God's call with the words, "Speak, for your servant hears." Samuel listened to God. Like Samuel, we must listen to

God. If we are his people, it means our hearts have been awakened by his Word. His Word is what shapes and conforms us. Do you listen eagerly to the Word of God? Do you anticipate the next week's sermon? One member of my church takes notes each Sunday and then reviews them Monday morning before work. That is an eager listener. Another family on Saturday nights reads the passage we are going to study the next morning. They are eager to hear God's Word. What about you? Do you open your Bible hungry to hear God speak? Do you go to church eager to learn and grow?

Samuel's first official act as a prophet was to denounce his mentor's family to his mentor's face (v. 18). He was initially afraid to tell Eli the vision, but his fear did not stop him. He still submitted to the Word of God and delivered the message God had given him. God's people do not simply listen to his Word; we listen and submit to it. We are hearers and doers, even though we are often called to do difficult things. Samuel became a prophet who unified Israel (v.19-21). From Dan, the extreme northern point of Israel, to Beersheba, the extreme southern point of Israel, it was clear to everyone that God had establish Samuel as his prophet (v. 20). Up to this point in Israel's history, the word "established" had only been used of Moses. Clearly, God had big plans for Samuel!

In the big picture of God's redemptive work, Samuel would play a vital role not only as a prophet who delivered the Word of God to the people of God, but also as a maker of kings. It was Samuel who anointed Saul as the first king of Israel. It was Samuel who visited Jesse from Bethlehem, met his sons, and then was told by

God's people respond to God's Word by listening.

> *Eli stands as warning about the danger of failing to listen to God's Word.*

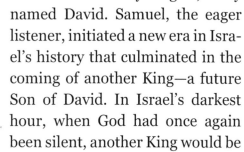

God to anoint the youngest, a boy named David. Samuel, the eager listener, initiated a new era in Israel's history that culminated in the coming of another King—a future Son of David. In Israel's darkest hour, when God had once again been silent, another King would be born in Bethlehem. This King would not only be the Son of David, but also the Son of God. This King would conquer mankind's greatest enemies. This King will one day return to establish an eternal kingdom where he will dwell with his people. The obedience of a little boy in the temple sparks a providential chain of events which culminates in the coming of Jesus Christ. Samuel, the kingmaker, causes us to look ahead to Jesus, the King.

Eli stands as warning about the danger of failing to listen to God's Word. Samuel, in contrast, serves as an example of eagerly listening and then obeying God's commands. But Eli and Samuel are not the only two characters in this drama. Who called Samuel? Who initiated the conversation? God did. We take for granted the astounding truth that God has revealed himself. The God of the universe came down to meet a young boy serving in the tabernacle. The God who spoke the world into existence, quietly spoke to a sleeping child. Our God is not a distant deity. He has made himself known. On our own, we could never know God. An ant has a better chance of learning calculus than we have of discovering God, and as created beings. we are far closer to an ant than to God. But God did not leave it to us. His self-revelation was our only hope of knowing him. We could have never reasoned our way to him for he is far too great and glorious for our feeble minds to even imagine.

His call of "Samuel! Samuel" reminds us of his self-revelation in the past (v. 10). Abraham was about to sacrifice his only son on the mountaintop. "But the angel of the LORD called to him from heaven and said, 'Abraham, Abraham!' And he said, 'Here am I (Gen 22:11).'" Jacob was about to take his family to Egypt. "And God spoke to Israel in visions of the night and said, 'Jacob, Jacob.' And he said, 'Here am I (Gen 46:2).'" Moses was called to lead God's people out of Egypt. "When the LORD saw that he turned aside to see, God called to him out of the bush, 'Moses, Moses!' And he said, 'Here I am (Ex 3:4).'" On each occasion, God intervened. He came down and made himself known to his people. God makes himself known to his people through his Word.

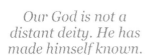

> *Our God is not a distant deity. He has made himself known.*

The reason God's people listen and submit to God's Word is because we find him there. The goal of preaching, teaching, and personal Bible reading is never to accumulate knowledge—the goal is to encounter God. The person who claims to love God but does not listen to his Word is like the husband who claims to love his wife but lives alone. If you do not listen to God's Word, then you do not love God. How did the Lord appear at Shiloh (v. 21)? He appeared through his Word. God's people listen and submit to God's Word because they love him, and he reveals himself in his Word. The apostle John wrote, "That which we have seen and heard we proclaim also to you, so that you too may have fellowship with us; and indeed our fellowship is with the

> *The goal of preaching, teaching, and personal Bible reading is never to accumulate knowledge—the goal is to encounter God.*

Father and with his Son Jesus Christ. And we are writing these things so that our joy may be complete (1Jn 1:3–4)." Through the Word of God, we have fellowship with God himself. Through the Word of God, our joy in him becomes complete. Let us then, like Samuel, be eager to listen and submit to God's Word.

Food for Thought Because God is our King, he has the authority to command us to do hard things. In those difficult moments, do you submit to his Word? When the Word of God reveals a painful step of obedience, do you take it? When Scripture exposes an area of sin, do you confess it or ignore the conviction? God's people should be identifiable by their eagerness to listen and their willingness to submit to God. The believer's posture is a cupped ear and a bent knee.

Faith in Action

Evaluate how eagerly you listen to God's Word. On a piece of paper make three columns with the headings Personal, Home, and Church. In each column, list ways you are listening to God's Word. Does one of these areas need more attention? Brainstorm some proactive steps you can take to be a more eager listener in each of these three areas.

Prayer

Read Psalm 19 and praise God for revealing himself to you both in creation and in the Bible. Turn the verses into statements of gratitude—i.e. "Thank you, Father, for your perfect law which has revived my soul (v.7)." End your time of prayer by praying verse 14 as you think about today's appointments, activities, and events.

Can God Be Trusted?

1 Samuel 4:1–22

Why do you listen to certain people? Is it because of their credentials? Is it due to their experience? Is it your relationship to them? Is it their position of authority? Every day we make decisions about who we allow to speak into our lives. Will I get my news from CNN or Fox? Will I choose my weather report from Channel 5 or Channel 11? Whether we consciously consider it or not, we have a set of criteria we use to choose whether to listen to someone or ignore them. The people we listen to have given us a reason to listen to them. It may be a good reason or a bad reason, but we have a reason.

The last chapter focused on two men: Eli and Samuel. Eli, the spiritual leader of Israel, was blind and deaf to the Word of God. Samuel, however, was eager to listen and submit to God's Word. The chapter ended on a high note with God revealing himself to Samuel at Shiloh. God was again speaking to his people. He was leading Israel through the word of his prophet. The dark days of the Judges seemed to be over.

All Israel recognized that Samuel was a prophet (v. 1). They understood that God had raised up a prophet to

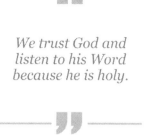

proclaim his Word, and through the word of this prophet God was going to govern his people. Sadly, although they recognized Samuel as a prophet, they did not listen to Samuel. They disregarded the Word of God. No mention is made of Samuel leading the people into battle, even though God was clearly speaking to him and all the people acknowledged it. We can draw no other conclusion than that the leaders of Israel did not want to listen to God's Word. God was clearly speaking to Samuel, but they chose to go into battle without asking Samuel if it was God's will. Through their failure to listen and obey, God's character was revealed, and we uncover three reasons to trust God and listen to his Word.

The first reason we trust God and listen to his Word is because he is holy. The Israelites were encamped at a place called Ebenezer and about to go into battle (v. 1). The word *Ebenezer* means "stone of help" and reappears in a significant way in chapter seven. It is ironic that they camped at the "stone of help," yet failed to go to the prophet of God and ask for God's help. The first battle was a terrible defeat. Four thousand troops lay dead on the battlefield. The leaders regrouped to figure out what went wrong and look for a way to achieve victory. They recognized God's sovereignty over the battle, but did not seek his guidance for their next engagement with the enemy (v. 3). They were defeated in battle because God was displeased with them, but they never sought to discover the source of his displeasure. They did not consult his prophet to determine why God caused the defeat. They asked the question "Why?" but did not wait for an answer, and then looked for a remedy through their own strength and wisdom. When Israel had been defeated in the battle in the past, the reason was always the same—a battlefield defeat was punishment for Israel's sin. They should have understood what was happening. The wickedness of the priests—Hophni and Phineas—was known by "all the people (2:23)." Yet, no one connected the dots.

Instead of turning to God and asking him for help, they called for the Ark of the Covenant to be brought from the temple (v. 4). The Ark of the Covenant was a carved wooden box, overlaid with gold, that contained the testimony God had given Moses. Carved on top of the box were cherubim—six-winged angels—whose wings covered the mercy seat on the lid. The Ark was the place where God met with Israel. It was normally located at the very center of the Tabernacle, and signified God's presence among his people. Notice carefully what the elders of Israel said, "Let us bring the Ark . . . that it may come among us and save us from the power of our enemies (v. 3)." Their response was little more than a scoop of superstition mixed with a heaping dose of idolatry. They had ignored the Word of God, overlooked sin, and now wanted the Ark to come and save them. Their view of God was no different than the pagan nations around them. They looked at God as a lucky charm that could mystically empower them in battle. If they could just march into battle with their idol leading the way, everything would be fine.

This is not the God of the Bible. The God of the Bible is a holy God. His holiness is his distinction from all created beings. His holiness means there is no one like him. The leaders of Israel ignored God's Word because they viewed God as nothing more

We trust God and listen to his Word because he is trustworthy.

We trust God and listen to his Word because he is sovereign.

than a man-made deity. They simply substituted an ark for a statue. Any sense of awe in his presence had been forgotten. They no longer remembered his majesty. God is the Lord of hosts (v. 4); the sovereign commander of heavenly armies. He is enthroned between the cherubim, ruling as king. Even though their enthusiasm for the Ark made the Philistines afraid (vv. 6–8), it ultimately furthered the Philistine's resolve (vv. 9–10). Israel suffered a great defeat because they failed to listen to God's Word. They treated God exactly like the pagan nations treated their man-made idols. They replaced the God of Israel with a golden box. If they had remembered the holiness of God (he alone is God and there is no one like him) and had listened to his Word, then this disaster could have been avoided.

The second reason we trust God and listen to his Word is because he is trustworthy. Earlier in 1 Samuel, God told Eli both of his sons would die on the same day (2:34). What God promised came to pass (v. 11). Whenever God makes a promise, it will happen. There is no possibility of failure, for nothing can prevent him from fulfilling his Word. With the defeat of Israel, the loss of the Ark, and the death of Eli and his two sons, God had done something which made the ears of Israel tingle. We see it in their reaction to the news of the messenger. The entire city cried out (v. 13). It had all happened exactly as God said it would.

The defeat and loss of life was because Eli failed to restrain his sons' wickedness. They were stealing the temple sacrifices, having sex with the temple servants, and causing the people to despise the place of worship. Eli was aware of their sin, but did not stop them. Here again we see Eli's unwillingness to deal with his sons. He was sitting on the edge of the city, waiting for news from the battle because "his heart trembled for the ark of God (v. 13)." Why was he so concerned? Because he knew the plan to take the Ark out to battle was foolish. But did he stop it? No. He again failed to perform his duty as the leader. He should have stopped them from bringing the Ark out to battle. The capture of the Ark was the result of his failure to check his sons' earlier behavior.

The third reason we trust God and listen to his Word is because he is sovereign. After the death of Eli and his sons, his daughter-in-law gave birth to a son and named him "Ichabod," which means "the glory has departed from Israel (v. 21)." God's glory—the awesome splendor of his invisible presence—had been exiled to another country. This chapter could read like the most depressing novel of all time. The entire priest's house was dead. Thirty-four thousand troops had been slaughtered. The army of Israel had disbanded. The Ark was gone. God had been exiled. What was going to happen to Israel? The situation was bleak. It appeared hopeless, but God had not given up. He was doing something. He answered Hannah's prayer. He spoke to Samuel. God was working. He had not deserted His people.

These events—the loss of the Ark and the departure of God's glory from Israel—did not catch God napping. He did not lose control. He did not fall asleep at the wheel of history. God was superintending every aspect of this picture. He was moving his presence out of Shiloh because he was going to make a different city his dwelling place. Every aspect had been orchestrated by God's hand as part of his plan to raise a king over Israel. Psalm 78 is an inspired recounting of these events and clearly shows that God would not be stopped. In fact, God was moving the center of his activity from Shiloh to Jerusalem. He was preparing the way for a king named David to care for his people. David was going to be a king who would also shepherd God's people. Even as the curtain closes on a dark chapter of Israel's history, we see that God is not silent. He speaks and his people listen and trust him.

The Israelites assumed God's favor and blessing could be earned by mechanical means, which is the same lie we believe when we think our performance earns God's approval. This is like expecting God to keep us healthy and well-fed because we are faithful to church. The only way for us to relate to God is through grace, never through works. No activity we do compels God to respond. No religious practice is a magic wand that wields God's power. God works in our lives by grace.

God has entrusted his reputation to his people. What does your example teach people about God? Do people get an accurate picture of him by watching you? Imagine a movie crew filmed the last week of your life and the footage was just released online. What would people think about God by watching you? What one thing would you most want them to know about God from observing your life?

Eli, the judge of Israel, was judged by the Judge of all the earth. God always judges sin. Confess your sin to God and trust his promise to forgive you. Ask him to reveal hidden sins and confess them as well. Praise God that because of Jesus, he can justly pardon you from the guilt of your sin.

An Epic Showdown

1 Samuel 5–6

The fifth chapter of 1 Samuel opens with an epic showdown in the temple of Dagon (5:1–2). Dagon was the supreme deity of the Philistines. In Judges 16, a blind Samson was brought into a feast for Dagon, celebrating Dagon's victory over Israel. You may remember how that story ended: Samson asked God for strength and collapsed the house, killing 3,000 Philistines who worshipped Dagon. Again, something from Israel was placed like a trophy in Dagon's trophy case. This time it was the Ark of God being displayed like a conquered relic. However, this trophy quickly became a liability. When Dagon's worshippers entered the temple the next day they discovered the idol lying on his face in humble submission to God (v. 3). The scene repeated itself the next morning, except this time Dagon's hands and feet were cut off. Hannah, Samuel's mother, had predicted this in her prayer. Describing God's power, she prayed, "The adversaries of the LORD shall be broken to pieces (2:10)." Here was a literal fulfillment. Dagon was not only bowing before God, but he had also been rendered completely powerless. He had been broken to pieces.

> *The more we give into sin, the more blind we grow to its utter foolishness.*

In contrast to Dagon who was lying limbless, God could still move his hands, and he did in such a way that the inhabitants of Ashdod became desperate to get rid of the Ark (vv. 6–7). The people said, "His hand is hard against us and against our god." Remember, the Ark was just a box, not a statue. Yet they attributed what was happening to God's hand, and they said all of this while the statue of their god was lying on the ground with its hands broken off. It is heartbreaking to see their blindness. How could they still consider Dagon their god? But that is what sin does. The more we give into sin, the more blind we grow to its utter foolishness.

The inhabitants of Ashdod sent the Ark to Gath, where the citizens of Gath were not excited to see the Ark roll into town. Any reservations were confirmed when the hand of the Lord came against the city, and tumors started to break out on the population (vv. 8–9). The Philistines realized the tumors were God's hand against them because of the Ark and wanted to get rid of it, so they sent it to Ekron. The presence of the Ark brought a panic of death in Ekron. People were dying, and those who were not dead were developing tumors. They were pleading for help, and their cries were so desperate that the sound reached heaven (vv. 10–12). This is rich with irony. Their cry reached heaven—the home of the God they had supposedly defeated. They were calling out for mercy to the foe they thought they had vanquished.

When the leaders of the Philistines called for the priests and diviners (or false prophets) they already knew what they wanted to do, they just did not know how to do it (6:1–2). They wanted to get rid of the Ark—to send it back to its own place. They were waving the white flag. They were acquiescing to the power of God and acknowledging their inability to control him. The priests cautioned them not to just send the Ark back, but to send an offering with it to appease God (vv. 3–6). Their words were an interesting syncretism of Old Testament instruction and pagan ritual. They made reference to three different truths from Israel's law—guilt offerings, the glory of God, and the exodus from Israel. However, despite their familiarity with the law, they violated it in three ways. First, they fashioned idols of mice and tumors—a violation of the second commandment. Second, the animal they selected—a mouse—was unclean (Lev 11:29). Finally, they placed the Ark of the Covenant on a cart to transport it, which was forbidden (Num 7).

More important is the parallel with an earlier account in Israel's history. Notice the similarities between the return of the Ark to Israel and the story of the Exodus. Both accounts begin with captivity in a foreign land, and the captivity is followed by plagues on the captors. As a result of the plagues, there is an exodus. In fact, the word translated "send away" in 6:3, can also be translated exodus, and is used throughout the story of the plagues in the book of Exodus. Moses used it before Pharaoh, and it is famously translated, "Let my people go." In the Exodus account, God told His people that when they left, they would not leave empty. Indeed, when they left Egypt, they left with carts filled with the gold and riches of their captors. In this account, the priests told the leaders not to return the Ark empty but to include treasures of gold.

The God who delivered his people from Egypt would deliver the Ark from the hand of the Philistines, and in the future would deliver his people from sin.

God's glory is seen in his grace.

The Philistine priests even mentioned the Exodus, instructing the leaders to not be like Pharaoh who hardened his heart against God. Finally, the captivity ended at a large stone in the field of Joshua with the Ark present, reminiscent of Joshua guiding the people across the Jordan, the Ark of God leading the way, and the people arranging twelve large stones as a memorial to God's deliverance. God works in the present and the future as he did in the past. The God who delivered his people from Egypt would deliver the Ark from the hand of the Philistines, and in the future would deliver his people from sin.

The Philistine leaders set up a test to confirm if the God of Israel was the one who had caused this to happen (vv. 7–9). They arranged a situation which should not have worked—they took two cows away from their calves and attached them to a wagon. These cows had never pulled a wagon before. If these cows were somehow able to bring the Ark to Israel it would confirm that the God of Israel had been behind all that took place. It worked and was a clear sign that God was doing it (vv. 10–12). The cows made sounds as if they wanted to return to their calves, but something kept them moving straight ahead. The cows took the Ark all the way to Israel, to the city of Beth-Shemesh (vv. 13–15). Israel did nothing to recapture the Ark. God did it, and he did it in such a way that everyone would know he did it. God does not need us, but in his grace, he uses us. He gives us the joy of serving him, but he is in no way dependent on us. Unlike Dagon, he does not need us to accomplish his purposes. The return of the Ark confirmed to the Philistine leaders that the God of Israel had brought this devastation on their cities and villages. They were glad to return this trophy (vv. 16–18).

In what should have been a time of rejoicing, Israel found itself mourning due to the tragic death of some of its people who treated the Ark improperly (vv. 19–21). At this moment in time, Israel was no different than the ungodly, unrighteous, thoroughly pagan nations around them. Just as the Philistines were ignorant of and disobedient to God's Word, so too were the Israelites. The condemning evidence was their response to the deaths of these men. They did not repent or confess their sin. Just like the Philistines, they sent the Ark of God away. They tried to get rid of it. Even with the return of the Ark, the prevailing spiritual atmosphere in Israel had not changed. God would need to blow the winds of revival through his people.

In this account from Israel's history, God's glory is revealed in his judgment of sin. Hannah said that God is a God of knowledge and "by him are actions weighed." He weighed the actions of the priests in chapter two and proclaimed a damning verdict. He weighed the actions of the Israelites in chapter four and brought a devastating defeat. He weighed the actions of the Philistines in chapter five and sent a deadly plague. He weighed the actions of the Bethshemeshites in chapter six and unleashed a destructive act. But God's glory is also seen in his grace. God was returning the Ark to his people. He had not given up on them. He had a plan for their salvation. This story is filled with judgment, but like a momentary break on a cloudy day, we see glimpses of hope. In the very next chapter, God uses his prophet to bring victory to his people. The triumphant return of the Ark sets the stage for a triumph in battle. God was again going to deliver Israel from the enemy.

Food for Thought The Philistines spoke the truth when they said, "Give glory to the God of Israel (6:5)." How did they make this conclusion? Twice in chapter five (vv. 6, 11), the author writes, "The hand of God was heavy" against the people. The word heavy shares the same root word as glory. They had experienced the heaviness of God through the heaviness of his hand of judgment. God's judgment reveals his glory. But God's judgment ultimately brings him glory by preparing the way for his grace.

Faith in Action

Centuries ago, John Calvin called the human heart an "idol-making factory." God alone is intrinsically glorious, but we constantly turn lesser things into idols. We glorify other things in place of God. The Philistines sought to glorify their god, Dagon, by building him an ornate temple and filling it with the trophies of conquered foes. How do you seek to glorify the true God? Are you building your life, your family, and your career to bring him glory?

Prayer

Ask God to help you live out the words of the apostle Paul: "Whether I eat or drink, or whatever I do, I will do all to the glory of God (1 Corinthians 10:31)." As you sit down to eat, pour your coffee, or drive to work, rehearse this prayer: "God, help me to do all things for your glory, not my own." When you get ready to sleep, review the main events of your day asking God to be glorified in both your successes and in your failures.

Repentance and Restoration

1 Samuel 7

Stories of restoration fill us with wonder because we live in a world marred by brokenness and crying out for restoration. The Bible addresses this need for restoration from cover to cover. It opens with the picture of a world that has not yet been broken, showing us what full restoration looks like. It explains why things are broken, and from the very opening pages, promises a way to be restored. The Bible also explains how all of these other broken, human relationships are actually symptoms of a deeper broken relationship—the relationship between God and man. We find hope as God makes a way for that fundamental relationship to be restored, and then reveals how that restoration is the gateway for all restoration. The Bible is one big story of restoration made up of many little stories of restoration. 1 Samuel seven is one of the little stories of restoration, and it can be a source of great instruction and great hope to all who live in this brokenness and long to see it restored.

> *Broken, human relationships are actually symptoms of a deeper broken relationship—the relationship between God and man.*

1 Samuel is set in the time of the Judges—a low point in Israel's history. Gone are the glorious victories under the leadership of Moses and Joshua, and in their place is a group of disorganized tribes, struggling with idolatry and foreign occupation. The spiritual leadership of Israel is almost non-existent. Their brokenness is thorough; it includes relationships, families, and government. The true source is sin, however, and they acknowledged it before God (v. 6). The people understood their need for restoration, and Samuel told them restoration begins with repentance. They needed a fundamental, drastic change in direction. Genuine repentance always includes three changes.

Genuine repentance first requires a change in affection. The whole nation of Israel longed for the Lord (v. 2). The word "longed" can also be translated "wailed, lamented, or grieved." You only wail, lament, and grieve if you have been cut-off from someone. They knew they had been cut-off from God, and they longed to be reconciled. They desired God and his presence. When the Ark was captured by the Philistines, one of Eli's daughters had a baby and named him *Ichabod*, which means, "the glory has departed from Israel (4:21)." God was gone. He had been cast aside by his people. They were cut off from him. But something began to stir inside them. Their affection for God changed, which lead to longing for him to return.

The change in Israel's affection for God was dramatic. Twenty years earlier, God struck down seventy Israelites who rebelled against his command and desecrated his holy Ark, and the people mourned (6:19). Then they asked how to get rid of the Ark. In chapter six they mourned because God had punished them and they wanted to get rid of him, but here in chapter seven they mourned because God was no longer with them. Their grief in chapter six was worldly grief over judgment for sin, but their grief in chapter seven was the kind that produced genuine repentance, because it began with a renewed affection for God.

A change in affection leads to a change in allegiance. If the Israelites were returning to the Lord, they needed to pledge allegiance to him alone, not to foreign idols. Samuel said worship "only him (v. 3)." What we love and live for is what we worship. What we give our time and talents to is what we worship. They had been giving their attention, their offerings, their sacrifices, and their allegiance to false gods, but in order to worship the Lord they had to get rid of them. Not partially, but totally.

Restoration begins with repentance, and repentance requires not only a change in affection and allegiance, but also a change in action. Feelings and declarations are great, but real repentance is demonstrated by one's actions. The natural outcome of repentance was participation in the God-given means of grace (vv. 4–6). They fasted and prayed, admitted their sin, and listened to Samuel. Their new allegiance was tested immediately. The Philistines heard that the nation of Israel had gathered together and assumed it was for battle, so they sent their army toward the Israelite gathering. Where would the Israelites turn for help? Would they turn back to their Baals and Ashtoreths? Would their repentance continue now that difficulty had come? They turned to God for help (vv .8–9). Their faith was in

Genuine repentance first requires a change in affection.

> A change in affection leads to a change in allegiance.

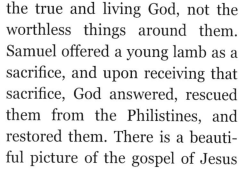

the true and living God, not the worthless things around them. Samuel offered a young lamb as a sacrifice, and upon receiving that sacrifice, God answered, rescued them from the Philistines, and restored them. There is a beautiful picture of the gospel of Jesus Christ in these events. A sinful people repent of their sin, they offer a lamb upon the altar, God receives the offering, and responds with rescue and restoration.

We see the change in Israel's spiritual condition when we compare their actions in chapter four with their actions in chapter seven. In chapter four, Israel tried to gain victory and deliverance through religious actions, and all it brought was failure and heartbreak. In chapter seven, the Israelites abandoned every effort to deliver themselves, and instead cried out to God based upon their restored relationship with him. He heard their cry and delivered them from the enemy in a supernatural way (v. 10). God won the victory. God brought deliverance. Salvation came through God's goodness and power, not their own.

When we forget what God has done for us, we easily slide back into sin. This is why God instituted so many feasts in the Old Testament. Each feast rehearsed a part of Israel's history and served as a reminder of his grace toward them, so that they would not fall back into sin. After the battle, Samuel set up a stone as a reminder of God's grace, and named it Ebenezer (v. 12). The name was significant for two reasons: first, the word *Ebenezer* means "the Lord has helped us." Second, the battle Israel had lost because they did not know God took place at a location named Ebenezer (ch. 4). This monument reminded Israel of their failure, and it also reminded them of God's grace.

The final few verses of the chapter summarize the life and ministry of Samuel, revealing the beauty of God's work of restoration in Israel. The Philistines were no longer in control of Israel, and they forfeited cities back to Israel that had previously been captured (vv. 13–14). Israel's repentance and God's restoration produced a time of peace unlike any the nation had ever known. Restoration follows repentance.

Restoration follows repentance.

Food for Thought Repentance always begins with a change in affection. Samuel commanded the people to return to the Lord with all their heart (v. 3). It is not enough to hate sin; we must also love God more than our sin. We must recognize his goodness and grace, see our sin as a failure to love him with all of our heart, and return to him with hearts of affection. Repentance is more than feeling bad about sin. Repentance is seeing sin as misplaced love and returning in whole-hearted love to the Father.

Faith in Action

Samuel commanded the people to serve God only (v. 3). Who do you serve? Look at last week's calendar. Where did you spend the majority of your time? Who was served by your schedule? Look at last month's bank statement. Where did you spend the majority of your money? Who was served by your paycheck? What simple change could you make this week to serve God with your time and money?

Prayer

Today you need to remind yourself of God's grace to you so your love for him grows. As your love for him grows, your sin looks less and less appealing. Affection for God is the most powerful deterrent to sin, and affection for God is where repentance begins. As you mediate on what Jesus has done, ask God to increase your affection for him.

Like the Other Nations

1 Samuel 8

Woven into the fiber of the American mindset is a distrust of monarchy. America has never had a king, and most Americans would involuntarily shudder at the thought of one. From the very start, Americans have rejected the concept of monarchy. Though my countrymen may not want a king, the spirit which gives rise to the desire for a king is one that is embedded in human nature. The desire for a king is really the desire for safety, protection, and security.

The chapter opens with a problem of leadership in Israel (v. 1), and the rest of the chapter unfolds Israel's solution to the problem. Along the way, it reveals who they trust to lead them. Like Eli before him, Samuel had two sons who follow him in his vocation, and these sons abused their position and acted wickedly. Samuel's sons were men who perverted justice and accepted bribes (v. 3). These sons—Joel, which means "Yahweh is God," and Abijah, meaning "My Father is Yahweh," did not walk in obedience and faith as Samuel did. The rest of the chapter

A godly leader does not guarantee a godly son.

is a series of conversations. Most are short, but one is a little longer. These conversations reveal not only the people's desire for a king, but also unveil the target of their trust.

The first conversation was between the people and Samuel. The leaders recognized a problem, but then offered a bewildering proposal (vv. 4–5). Back to back leaders had sons that were placed in positions of spiritual leadership by virtue of heredity, and the sons used their positions to extort the people and gain wealth for themselves. Their recent history clearly showed that a godly leader does not guarantee a godly son. But they asked for a king to be appointed. They asked for a monarchy to be established. They asked for a ruler to be put in place whose son would be replaced by his son and then his grandson, great-grandson, right on down the line. Based on their history, their request made no sense.

Why did they demand a king? They wanted a king so they would be like the other nations, but God's plan was never for his people to be like all the other nations. God told them repeatedly that they were to be a special, distinct nation. Just before God gave Moses the 10 Commandments, he had Moses tell Israel they were to be his "treasured possession," a "kingdom of priests and a holy nation (Ex 19:5–6)." God is not like other gods, so why should his people be like other nations? His people were to be holy, distinct, and set apart because they served a God who was holy, distinct, and set apart.

The next conversation was between Samuel and God (vv .6–9). God saw that Samuel was struggling with the people's rejection and reminded him that he was not the one being rejected; they were rejecting God. The reason God said they were rejecting him was because he was the King of Israel (Ex 15:18; Num 23:21; Deut 33:5; Judg 8:23). Their desire for a human king was a rejection of God's rule. The request for a human king was another chapter in Israel's history of idolatry.

Samuel replayed for the people his conversation with the Lord (vv. 10–18), informing them about the king's ways. The word translated "ways" of a king (v. 11) is the same word as "justice" in verse three and "customs" back in chapter two. In other words, the behavior of a king would be similar to the behavior of the second-generation leaders they had just witnessed. The king would be like the corrupt judges and wicked priests. Eli's sons took the best meat from the sacrifice when the people came to worship, and Samuel's sons took bribes from the rich when the people came to be judged. In similar ways, the king would take from the people he led. Instead of having someone to do justice for them, they would have a king to take from them. The king would take their sons (vv. 11–12), daughters (v. 13), land (v. 14), harvest (v. 15), workers (v. 16), and flocks (v. 17), and they would be his slaves (v. 17). They refused to listen to Samuel and persisted in their cry for a king. They wanted a king who would build a standing army, so they would not have to trust God to deliver them (vv. 19–20). They no longer wanted to be dependent on God to raise up a deliverer. They wanted a king to trust when an enemy attacked. They wanted a military leader who would fight their battles for them. How quickly they forgot the lessons from Ebenezer, where God fought their battle for them. God allowed them to have what they

Our greatest problem is trusting man instead of trusting God.

> *We trust man instead of God whenever our desires are shaped by the world instead of the Word.*

wanted and then sent them home (vv. 21–22). Samuel would do what they asked. He would anoint the king they wanted; a king like the other nations.

We have the same problem they had. Our greatest problem is trusting man instead of trusting God. We tend to think our biggest issue is one of obedience, and the problem lies in our lack of willpower. The problem is not our weakness, but our confidence in our own strength. The Israelites wanted to have a king they could trust, but God's plan was to give them a leader who would lead them to trust him. How did Israel move away from trusting God and seeing his great deliverance (ch. 7) to asking for a king to replace God (ch. 8)? They looked at the other nations, saw they had a king, and wanted one for themselves. Then they refused to listen to the prophet (v. 19). How do we move from trusting God to trusting man? We trust man instead of God whenever our desires are shaped by the world instead of the Word. The more our ears grow deaf to Scripture, the more our faith will be rooted in what we can see. But the more receptive we are to God's Word, the deeper our confidence sinks in the eternal God.

If our greatest problem is trusting man, then our greatest need is to trust God. We learn to trust God by remembering that he has worked in the past, he is working in the present, and he will work in the future. The previous chapter records a great victory for Israel when God thundered from heaven, confusing the Philistines and delivering them into the hands of Israel. At the end of the battle, Samuel took a rock and named it Ebenezer, which meant "stone of help", so that Israel would remember what God had done. Their past was a living history of God's working for their good. But God was also working in their present. The next three chapters chronicle the choice of Saul as king over Israel. Saul was chosen because they wanted a king like the other nations. Saul was a mighty warrior. He was courageous, but he also did whatever he wanted to do. God chose Saul in the present to reveal the foolishness of the people's request. But God was also preparing another king, a shepherd boy named David. He would not be a king like the kings of other nations. He would be a king whose heart was after God's heart. He would be a king who led the people to trust God as their ultimate king. In all these events, God was working in their present situation, and God would work in their future. God promised a king would come who was the son of Abraham and the son of David. Israel was to trust this coming King—a King unlike any other King. This King does not make God's people like other nations, instead he draws subjects from all nations to come and worship him. In this King, Jesus Christ, we find true safety and security. For this King has conquered death and reigns forevermore.

Our greatest need is to trust God.

Food for Thought God allowed the Israelites to have what they desired, even though what they desired was not best for them (v.22). We often grow frustrated and angry when God tells us "No", even though God's "No" is always for our good. If we knew what was best for us, we would never want God to give us what we want. We would always ask God to give us what he wants for us.

Faith in Action

The power of our testimony as God's people is tied directly to the distinctiveness of our lives. People will not be drawn to Christ if you live exactly like them; people will be drawn to Christ if they see the difference Christ makes in your life. Like Israel, do you desire conformity to the world, or do you embrace your position as one set apart for God's use?

Prayer

When Samuel was frustrated, he turned to God in prayer (v. 6). Are you frustrated with a situation in your life? Are you frustrated with a person in your life? We often turn to other people to share our frustrations. Instead share your frustrations with God right now. Cast those frustrations on the one who is strong enough to carry them (1 Pet 6:7).

God Is Not Weightless

1 Samuel 9

"It is one of the defining marks of Our Time that God is now weightless." David Wells wrote this devastating critique in his book *God in the Wasteland*. He explained: "I do not mean by this that he is ethereal but rather that he has become unimportant. He rests upon the world so inconsequentially as not to be noticeable. He has lost his [importance] for human life. Those who assure the pollsters of their belief in God's existence may nonetheless consider him less interesting than television, his commands less authoritative than their appetites for affluence and influence, his judgment no more awe-inspiring than the evening news, and his truth less compelling than the advertisers' sweet fog of flattery and lies. That is weightlessness" (David F. Wells, *God in the Wasteland: The Reality of Truth in a World of Fading Dreams,* Eerdmans, p. 88).

More than two decades after he offered this analysis, it still rings true. While spiritual language has grown more fashionable, God has actually been pushed further from the center of our existence. More people mention God's

> *The transcendent Creator God is actively working to bring about his purposes in his world.*

name while simultaneously ignoring him than ever before. We have become masters at perpetuating a godliness that exists completely separate from God. Babies are dedicated, children are baptized, church is attended, tithes are given, membership is enlarged, and God is ignored.

Christianity teaches about a God who is all-knowing, all-powerful, and transcendent, while at the same time he is present, personal, and caring. But that reality is messy. It can be uncomfortable. It is certainly humbling. It is much easier to make God an impersonal force in the sky, a sanitized version of the Force, or a big man upstairs. Or to go the opposite direction and make Jesus your homeboy, your invisible buddy, or your personal spiritual guru. In both cases, the heaviness of God is lost, and we perpetuate the myth that God is weightless.

1 Samuel nine provides a much needed reality check. It does not jive with the weightless God embraced in modern-day religion. Instead it shows us an accurate picture of the God who actually is. It rejects the caricature of God as a distant deity or a cuddly homeboy, and instead shows us that the transcendent Creator God is actively working to bring about his purposes in his world. We are first introduced to Saul in chapter nine. Though this chapter reveals a great deal about Saul, it reveals even more about God.

In our first introduction to Saul, we learn he came from a wealthy, prominent family (v. 1). Saul was a very handsome man; the most handsome man in Israel. He was also exceptionally tall (v. 2). In other words, Saul looked the part of a leader. Tall, handsome, and wealthy, he looked exactly like a king should. Even his name was significant, because the name "Saul" means "the one requested." How appropriate. The people had requested a king, and God was going to answer that request with Saul. Saul was sent by his father to look for some lost donkeys (v. 3). What a strange way to begin the story of Israel's first king. But something as trivial as lost donkeys led to something momentous. Even in the smallest of details, like lost donkeys, God was working to accomplish his plan.

The story takes an interesting twist as Saul runs into a "man of God (vv. 5—10)." Though the man of God is not yet named in the story, we recognize him as Samuel. Saul does not, which provides another clue about Saul. He was physically imposing, but spiritually ignorant. Just a few chapters earlier, we were told that all Israel recognized Samuel as a prophet (3:20). But Saul seemed completely unaware of his existence.

Without context, the story up to this point seems insignificant—a rich family lost their donkeys, and their son had trouble finding them. The son's servant thought they should ask a prophet where the donkeys had gone. It appeared inconsequential, but we know there was more happening behind the scenes, because the previous chapter ended with God obliging the people's request for a king. We also learn what God told Samuel the previous day that he would send a man from Benjamin to see him, and this man should be anointed king (vv. 15–16). When Samuel saw Saul, God confirmed that he was the one (v. 17). God had sent Saul to Samuel. The donkeys were not lost; they were divinely led away. God had chosen Saul to be king over his people and would use Saul to deliver them from their enemies. Though God was install-

God was giving them a king, but he was not giving them to the king.

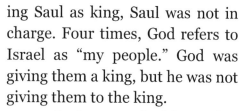

> *God is both transcendent and present.*

ing Saul as king, Saul was not in charge. Four times, God refers to Israel as "my people." God was giving them a king, but he was not giving them to the king.

Saul approached Samuel to ask him directions to the prophet's house (v. 18). Not only did Samuel reveal that he was the prophet, but he had news for Saul that would cause his jaw hit to the floor. Samuel invited Saul to dinner, assured him the donkeys were safe, and proceeded to tell Saul that everything desirable in Israel was going to be his (vv. 19–20). Saul's response was one of shock: Who am I? Why have you told me this (v. 21)? The surprises continued. Saul arrived at the party as the guest of honor (v. 22). He was put at the head of the table and given the choicest piece of meat. The meal may have been a surprise to Saul, but it was not to Samuel. God had told Samuel was what going to happen. God had planned every event, from the lost donkeys to the dinner party.

In this account we are assured that God is both transcendent and present. We make God weightless whenever we hold to one attribute without the other. If we affirm that God is sovereign, omnipresent, and far above us, while denying that he is active in our lives, then we turn him into an impersonal force. He becomes the big guy up above who moves us like pawns on a global chess board. On the other hand, if we deny his transcendence and simply talk about his activity with us, he becomes a helpful advisor or a co-pilot who dispenses sage advice. Both of these caricatures of God—the distant deity

> *We make God weightless whenever we hold to one attribute without the other.*

and the perky advisor—open the door for us to push him out. They begin the process of making him unimportant.

> *Both of these caricatures of God—the distant deity and the perky advisor—open the door for us to push him out.*

This account in Saul's life does not allow us to minimize God's sovereign power over all things or his active presence in this world. We see his transcendent power as he orchestrates every event and arranges every detail—even lost donkeys. But we also see that God is present. He speaks to Samuel. He encourages Saul through multiple signs. He is both transcendent and present. The God of the universe is our God. He is reigning over the starry hosts, while at the same time he is loving, listening, and speaking to his people.

Food for Thought Since God is both transcendent and imminent, he is able to hold the entire universe in his hands at the same time he holds individual people. Isaiah wrote that God "will gather the lambs in his arms (40:11)," and with those same arms he is able to measure the heavens (40:12). Only someone infinitely glorious can be present everywhere yet still be personally available to his people whenever they call.

Faith in Action

The same God who orchestrated the movements of donkeys in Saul's day is still orchestrating events in your life today. No detail in the life of one of his people is too insignificant for God to know about and care about. Write a note of encouragement to another Christian who needs to be reminded of God's sovereign goodness and personal care.

Prayer

As is evident in Saul's life, God is active on both national and personal levels. He is orchestrating events around the globe and in individual lives. Pick three nations where the Gospel is relatively unknown and pray for God to begin a mighty work there. Now pick three people who have not believed the Gospel and pray for God to begin a saving work in them.

The King Confirmed

1 Samuel 10–11

Chapter ten opens with Saul being anointed by the prophet Samuel (v. 1). The purpose of someone being anointed was to signify that this person was being set aside for God's special use. There was nothing magical about Samuel's flask of oil. What as special was God's activity. Twice in the first verse Samuel told Saul, "The Lord anointed you." The anointing with oil symbolized God's choice of Saul. He was making a divine claim on Saul. While the oil flowed out of the jar and onto Saul's head it was a picture of the Spirit of God flowing down and enabling Saul in his new role as Israel's leader. Though Saul was being installed as Israel's prince, Israel would still be God's people. Samuel called the people God's "heritage;" they were literally his "permanent possession."

Saul was given three signs to confirm Samuel's words (vv. 2—8). Each sign repeated something that happened earlier to Saul. First, he would meet someone who quoted back to him his own words about the donkeys. Then he would be given gifts of bread, since he and his servant had no bread in their sacks. Finally, just as he discovered Samuel earlier, he would find prophets coming

While the oil flowed out of the jar and onto Saul's head it was a picture of the Spirit of God flowing down and enabling Saul in his new role as Israel's leader.

down from a high place. Why give him all these signs? The reason was to confirm God's message to Saul. They were to bring Saul confidence that God's Word through his prophet could be trusted. The King of Israel was to lead the people to obey God, and God would instruct the king through the prophet. From the start, God was teaching Saul to trust his Word. God's Word through Samuel was confirmed. Each sign played out as God said it would. It happened in such a remarkable, unexpected way that a new saying—"Is Saul also among the prophets?"— was developed whenever something surprising happened (v. 11).

Seven days after Saul left, Samuel gathered the people at Mizpah, the location of God's great victory over the Philistines (ch.7). Before revealing the king, he reminded them that God had been their king and given them great victories, but they had chosen to reject him (vv. 18—19). In this very spot where God had delivered them, they rejected him. The tribes were brought before Samuel, and when he cast lots, the tribe of Benjamin was selected. The next lot fell upon the clan of the Matrites from all the clans of Benjamin, and the final lot fell upon Saul of all the sons of Kish. These details not only add spice to the account, they also remind us that God was in control of every detail. The casting of lots excluded human choice and relied completely on God's will. Even after Saul was chosen, the people could not find him. They had to ask God where their new king could be found. They may have had a new king, but God was still on the throne.

This choosing of Saul reached its climax with a couple of significant revelations. First, the king was still under God's law, because the rights and duties of the kingship were given by God (v. 25). Second, Saul appeared to be a great candidate (v. 23). He was humble; he certainly was not seeking the position of king. He was strong—stronger and taller than everyone else. His future failure as a king could not be traced to his qualifications. He met all of the criteria the people wanted. His future failure as a king was for another reason—he would fail to obey the Word of God through the prophet.

Not long after Saul was confirmed as king, the Israelite city of Jabesh-gilead was besieged by the Ammonites (11:1). They were going to be taken as slaves and disgraced in such a way that all of Israel would feel it. The leaders of the city asked the Ammonites for permission to send out messengers for help. If no help came in seven days, they would surrender (v. 3). The enemy believed Israel was so weak that they allowed Jabesh-gilead to send out the messenger. The Spirit of God moved on Saul when he heard about the distress of Jabesh-Gilead, and he responded as a king should. He rallied the people to defend their fellow countrymen (vv. 4—7). God worked in Saul to transform him from a farmer to a warrior. Through Saul, God gave Israel a great victory. He delivered Jabesh-gilead from the hands of the Ammonites (vv. 8—11). Saul was not only gracious in victory, but he was also merciful to those who had opposed Him (vv. 12—13). He refused to punish those who had publicly questioned his position as king.

They may have had a new king, but God was still on the throne.

The long story of the selection and revelation of Israel's first

A brave and powerful leader is not always a godly one.

king concludes with the people ascribing victory to the Lord and offering sacrifices of thanksgiving (vv. 14—15). The story began with Saul, a man hunting for donkeys who found a kingdom, and it ends with Saul, now a valiant and mighty deliverer. But what happens in the coming chapters is that Saul's great beginning has a tragic ending. A brave and powerful leader is not always a godly one.

The book of 1 Samuel constantly pushes us to look past the immediate events to something beyond. It is as if the writer was writing about events that took place on a little hill, but behind the little hill was a grand mountain. Each event on the little hill introduced a similar event on the grand mountain.

On the little hill Israel was given a king, but our attention is drawn to the mountain where God's Son is born as the ultimate king. Israel's first king is anointed, and we look toward the Anointed One who reigns over all creation. Israel's first king is victorious over the enemy, and we see Jesus Christ triumphing over sin, death, and hell. The context of these events reveals God's grand story of redemption—a story with universal ramifications. Yet, we also see God was working in individual lives. The clearest statement is in 10:9: "When [Saul] turned his back to leave Samuel, God gave him another heart." The grand story is a personal story. God sent his son as the ultimate king, and that king delivers his people one at a time. This statement of a new heart is part of a larger promise God made, a promise called the New Covenant. God promised that the death of Jesus Christ for the sin of mankind would inaugurate the New Covenant, a way of God relating to man, not by works but by faith. Instead of an external law with all of its rules and regulations, God would give his people new hearts; hearts that had the law written on them. With these new hearts, God's people would be able to serve their king in his kingdom forever.

God sent his son as the ultimate king, and that king delivers his people one at a time.

Food for Thought

Our hope, like the citizens of Jabesh-Gilead long ago, is not in our own strength. We are trapped by an enemy that wants to destroy us, and our only hope is to ask our king for help. Just as King Saul came to free his people from impending slavery and possible death, Jesus came to free his people from slavery to sin and eternal death. Our hope is not in our strength or cunning, but in our king's power and might.

Faith in Action

Divide a piece of paper into two columns. At the top of the left column write the word "Hopes," and at the top of the right put the word "Hero." List your hopes in the left column, and in the right put the name of the person you are trusting to make that hope come true. If your hopes are all in people, you will be disappointed. Our hope needs to be in Jesus.

Prayer

Think of those in your church who are struggling with fear, anxiety, and hopelessness. Insert their name into Paul's prayer and pray it for them: "May the God of hope fill _____ with all joy and peace in believing, so that by the power of the Holy Spirit _____ may abound in hope" (Romans 15:13).

Rejecting the Real King

1 Samuel 12:1–18

On March 4, 1865, Abraham Lincoln addressed a country divided by civil war. His second inaugural address was a mere 701 words. There were no memorable lines, but there were plenty of wise words. Lincoln stood before the people and calmly assessed the problem encompassing the nation, and then offered a solution to propel the wounded nation forward. He began by recounting what had led them to this point in history, but he did not end there. He did not merely diagnose the problem—he offered a solution. He pointed ahead to a remedy. He highlighted a path forward. The final words of his speech were: "With malice toward none, with charity for all, with firmness in the right as God gives us to see the right, let us strive on to finish the work we are in, to bind up the nation's wounds, to care for him who shall have borne the battle and for his widow and his orphan, to do all which may achieve and cherish a just and lasting peace among ourselves and with all nations." There was a way forward. There was a reason

> *Samuel was not their problem, and neither was their previous system of government.*

for hope. The mistakes of the past could be fixed. That was Lincoln's message.

The nation of Israel was in a very similar predicament. They were not engaged in a civil war; in fact they just won a great victory over another nation (ch. 11). But they had made a terrible mistake, and the question stretched out before them was how they would respond. In 1 Samuel 12, the aging prophet Samuel, stood up before the nation to install the new king. It was the inaugural address, not from the incoming king, but from the seasoned prophet. In his speech, he described the nation's problem and delivered the necessary solution. In his address, we find hope for our failures, wisdom for our mistakes, and grace for our sins.

The nation's problem was not Samuel. As an old man, he stood before them and gave them an opportunity to publicly rebuke him for failure as their leader (vv. 1—3). Yet, no one could say anything against him (v. 4). He even gave them specific areas to consider, areas where leaders often fail. "Did I use my position to gain wealth? Did I take bribes or accept kickbacks? Was I unjust in my judicial decisions? Did I ever abuse my power?" He had not. Samuel was not their problem, and neither was their previous system of government. Samuel was appointed by God to be their judge. He was God's chosen leader for the people. If no charges could be brought against him, then no charges could be brought against the previous form of administration.

Was the problem how the Lord had dealt with the nation? Of course not. Like a lawyer, Samuel was going to make a case that the Lord's deeds had always been righ-

teous (vv. 6–7). The nation's problems could not be traced back to
Samuel, the system of judges, or
the Lord. Samuel recounted the
righteous deeds of the Lord. He
began with God's work of rescuing
them from slavery in Egypt and
bringing them into the Promised

*Each time the people
called for help, God
raised up a judge to
bring deliverance.*

Land (v. 8). Once in the Promised Land, the people sinned
greatly by forgetting the Lord, so God delivered them into
the hand of the Philistines (v. 9). The people repented,
called out for God to help, and God raised up a judge to
rescue them from their captivity (vv. 10–11). This cycle
was repeated: rebellion, captivity, repentance, and deliverance. Each time the people called for help, God raised
up a judge to bring deliverance. If the problem before the
nation was not Samuel, the Judges, or God, what was it?

The problem was the people's rejection of God's
rule (v. 12). Instead of submitting to God and trusting him
to protect them, they looked at the nations around them,
and similarly wanted a king. In fact, it was the pagan king
attacking them that inspired their desire for a king. Their
problem was that God was not enough for them. They wanted something different. They wanted something more.

You can almost hear the irony drip off of Samuel's statement in verse 13: "Look at your king whom you
have chosen…" After recounting
God's repeated work of salvation,
which included supernatural acts
and spanned generations, Samuel
pointed to a lone human and basically said, "Here he is. Here's the
one you wanted instead of God."
He concluded his indictment with

*Their problem was
that God was not
enough for them.*

Every sin you commit is a rejection of God's rule.

the phrase: "behold, the LORD has set a king over you (v. 13)." Oh, the foolishness of the people! In rejecting God as king, they had to ask God for a king. How could this king be a greater king than God, if God was the one who chose him and appointed him?

Their rejection of God as king was significant, and Samuel wanted them to understand the enormity of the problem. So, in the middle of the dry season, Samuel prayed and a thunderstorm swept the earth (vv. 16—18). It was an object lesson no one there would forget. As the thunder crashed around them, they were reminded that God's wrath would thunder upon the guilty. As the lightning struck the earth, they were reminded that God's judgment would strike those who had sinned. As the rain poured down, they were reminded that God's fury would be poured out on those who rebelled.

Do you realize that every sin you commit is a rejection of God's rule. Every time you tell a lie, speak an unkind word, , hold a grudge, share some gossip, take a lustful look, or boast about yourself, you are rejecting God's rightful rule as King and committing an act of treason. Every sinful decision is an act of war. You are deposing the King and assuming his throne. When you disobey the King's command, you are telling him that he has no claim over you. You are defying his law and rebelling against his authority. The problem facing the nation of Israel is a problem facing each one of us—we have asked for a different king—and the judgment facing the nation of Israel is a judgment facing each one of us as well.

Food for Thought The foolishness of rejecting God's rule was not unique to the Israelites. Their problem is shared by all humanity. We have rebellion woven into our DNA. Why did Israel want a king? They wanted greater security and greater status. If you are a Christian, is your security in Christ enough or do you look for security in other things? Is your status as a child of God enough or do you need a title as well?

Faith in Action

Every morning that you wake up, you face a choice about your allegiance. If we are honest, many days begin with us reciting the pledge of allegiance to our desires: "I pledge allegiance to myself, and to the plans and dreams for which I stand. One motive, under me, for the enjoyment and pleasure of myself alone." Instead of starting the day swearing allegiance to your wishes, start today committing yourself fully to God and his rule in your life.

Prayer

Pray a prayer of allegiance to God today using the words of Proverbs 3:5-6: "Lord, help me not to trust myself and my desires but to trust you without reservation. In every situation and with every decision, help me to acknowledge your rule and reign, knowing that you alone can lead me in straight paths."

Whole-Hearted Allegiance

1 Samuel 12:19–25

Israel had rejected the rule and reign of God in favor of a human king. Now that Samuel had confronted them with their rebellion, what was the solution? How should Israel respond to the condition they were in—a condition which resulted from their rebellious decision? Samuel offered them a path forward with three simple commands: follow the Lord, do not turn aside, and remember his works.

Samuel's first command was to follow the Lord. He used a number of different words—fear, serve, obey, and listen—but all of them focus on the matter of allegiance. Return your allegiance to God. Stop looking for a new king to follow. Stop rebelling against his rule. Swear fidelity to your King. Serve in his kingdom. Listen to his decrees. Obey his laws. God requires our whole-hearted allegiance. Our short-term pleasures and short-sighted plans must be cast aside, replaced by whole-hearted commitment to God. Twice in this speech, Samuel exhorted the people to follow the Lord "with all your heart (vv. 20, 24)." God demands

Half-hearted commitment brings whole-hearted misery.

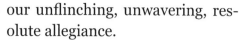

our unflinching, unwavering, resolute allegiance.

We like to give pieces of our heart away, but not the entire thing. We give God a piece of our heart on Sunday but keep the rest throughout the week. We give him a piece in public while keeping other parts private. We offer God the guest room, but tell him the master suite is off-limits. We offer 10% of our money and then keep 90% for ourselves. Samuel's commands do not allow for partial allegiance. Can a servant choose to only obey his master at certain times? Can a soldier follow his general merely when its convenient? Can a citizen obey just the laws he likes? No man can serve two masters. Half-hearted commitment brings whole-hearted misery.

Samuel's first command was to follow the Lord, and his second was to not turn aside (vv. 20—21). Why would anyone turn aside from following the Lord? More specifically, why would they turn aside after empty things? When we say it that way, it seems so simple: "How stupid to turn aside from following God to purse empty things!" But we forget they are empty until we have gone after them.

In 1991, a man sued a beer company for $10,000 for false advertising. He claimed to suffer from emotional distress (in addition to mental and physical injury), because when he drank beer, he did not have any luck with the ladies like the television ads promised. He also did not like that he got sick sometimes after he drank. As we follow the Lord, we are besieged with false advertising. Empty things that distract us from whole-hearted allegiance to Christ do not advertise themselves that way. They promise us one thing—like luck with the ladies—and give us something else—like vomiting in a toilet. The Israelites turned aside from following God to pursue false gods and human saviors (vv. 10, 13). What were they looking for? They were looking for someone who could bless them and someone who could save (v. 21).

The one who turned aside after false gods would not be saved, but be swept away (v. 25). Samuel used the metaphor *swept away* right after sending a thunderstorm. What a frightening image! What a contrast with the one who follows God and receives the promise that "it will be well (v. 13)." What a fearful thing to be swept away in a storm of judgment. This image is reminiscent of Jesus' parable about the foolishness of building your life on anything other than his words. The one who turns to something other than Jesus for his foundation will see his life crumble during the storm (Mt 7:24—27). Samuel commanded the people to follow the Lord and not turn aside.

The third command from Samuel was to consider God's works. How do we keep from turning aside with all of the false advertising around us? How do we follow God with our whole heart? We must consider all the wonderful works God has done on our behalf (v. 24). Faith and gratitude motivate obedience. Faith assures us that God fulfills his promises, and gratitude reminds us we are the recipients of those fulfilled promises. If you want encouragement to follow God, then reflect upon the great things he has done in your life. He loved you enough to send his only begotten Son, so if you believe on him you will not perish but have eternal life.

Faith and gratitude motivate obedience.

The type of reflection necessary may require you to slow down. You might be so busy with

If you want encouragement to follow God, then reflect upon the great things he has done in your life.

good things that you do not have time to stop and consider the great things God has done for you. If you never slow down, then do not be surprised when you find yourself embracing one of the empty gods of this world. One of our greatest challenges as believers is remembering what God has done. We are so forgetful. God works, and we forget. Samuel commanded the people to "stand still and see this great thing (v. 16)." We need to listen to Samuel's instruction. Like the Israelites, we grow comfortable with our sin in large part because we never stop to consider what great things the Lord has done. Remembering brings repentance. Considering brings confession. If you want to follow the Lord, then be intentional about reflecting on his greatness. Be deliberate about considering his great works in your life. Time spent reflecting on God's work in your life serves as a guardrail to keep you on the right path.

What happens when you put a child who loves candy in a candy store, tell them not to touch anything, and then leave? Eventually, they will touch something. Some of them resist for a long time, and some for very little time. But eventually the temptation is too great. This feels similar to our predicament. We live in a world filled with advertisements for false gods. What hope is there for us to keep following the Lord when we are constantly assaulted by false advertisements?

Our hope does not rest in our own effort. Our hope is not rooted in our own strength. Our

Remembering brings repentance. Considering brings confession.

hope is in the God who can bless and save (v. 22). Our hope is in the God who raised up Moses and Aaron, who called Israel out of Egypt, who delivered them from the Philistines, and who sent his Son to rescue us from sin and death. Our hope is that our God is faithful and

Our hope is in the God who can bless and save.

good. He will not forsake us. No matter the depth of our sin, the grace of our God is deeper still. In Jesus Christ— the true King—we find hope for every failure, wisdom for every mistake, and grace for every sin.

Food for Thought There is a battle being fought for your heart's allegiance (2 Cor 10:3—4). The enemy is tempting you to embrace rogue thoughts about the authority of God. He is assaulting you with arguments against the supremacy of Jesus Christ. He is inflating your view of yourself, hoping you will rebel against God's rule. What areas of your heart are you keeping as your own fiefdom? Can you identify where the enemy has built strongholds in your heart?

Faith in Action

Do something to intentionally consider God's great works in your life. Keep a journal. Write notes in your Bible or a devotional book like this. Establish traditions intended to prompt reflection. Send an email. Post on a blog. Write a letter. Take an evening by yourself. As you plant those memories deep in the soil of your heart, you will begin to see gratitude, faith, and allegiance bloom.

Prayer

Read Ephesians one and thank God for the amazing spiritual blessings that are yours in Jesus Christ. Pick out as many as you can—blessings like election, adoption, and redemption. As you thank him for these blessings, rehearse how each one has changed your life.

The Problem with Success Part 1

1 Samuel 13–14

A 2006 study conducted by *Success* magazine uncovered some surprising insights into the way Americans view success. In response to the phrase, "Success in business means...," 60% of the respondents selected, "Adding value to the lives of others." Less than 20% said success meant, "Making a lot of money (The New American Dream, *Success*, Summer 2006, p. 88)." Four years later this same magazine's five nominees for "Achiever of the Year" included Bill Gates, Warren Buffett, Steve Jobs, Oprah Winfrey, and Mark Zuckerberg, all of whom were billionaires.

At best, our society is sending mixed messages about true success. In today's passage, we discover that God's definition of success is clear and unchanging, and it is at odds with the definitions written on magazine headlines. What God views as successful is unlikely to bring you

> *There is nothing more important than aligning your view of success with God's.*

a nomination for "Achiever of the Year" from *Success* magazine, but there is nothing more important than aligning your view of success with God's. Is the success you seek in line with God's view of success? What informs your perspective on true success? Saul, Israel's first king, was a failure in God's eyes. As we observe his failure, we discover how God measures success and find a warning about seeking worldly achievements.

If success was based solely on outward achievements, then King Saul would have been deemed "Achiever of the Year." When he became king, the situation in Israel was dire. Israel's army was a measly three thousand men (v. 2). Throughout the country, their enemy, the Philistines, had built garrisons to oppress them. Jonathan, Saul's son, was victorious over one of the garrisons, but the result was that Israel had now become a stench in the nostrils of the Philistines (v. 4). In our terms, Israel to the Philistines was like a stinky diaper to the nursery workers. All the Philistines wanted was to dispose of the Israelites.

In contrast to Israel's three thousand man army, the Philistines had an army with thirty thousand chariots, six thousand horsemen, and infantry soldiers too vast to number (v. 5). When they amassed this army to attack Israel, the predictable response was discouragement and fear. Many of Saul's soldiers began to desert the army (vv. 6—7), and as a result, Saul's army dwindled down to six hundred men. Plus, the Philistines had begun to send out raiding parties; these parties would squash rebellion and prevent any additional troops from reaching Saul's meager force (vv.15—17).

Not only was Saul's army small, but also it was ill-equipped. The Philistines had removed all the blacksmiths from Israel to prevent them from making weapons (v. 19). As a result, the Israelites had to sharpen their farming equipment in an attempt to make them dangerous (vv. 20—21). Only Saul and Jonathan had swords. Has there been a more ill equipped army in human history? 600 men against thirty thousand chariots. Two swords against a well-stocked army. The odds were certainly not in Israel's favor. They appeared to stand little chance. But by the end of chapter 14, we find this outcome, "When Saul had taken the kingship over Israel, he fought against all his enemies on every side, against Moab, against the Ammonites, against Edom, against the kings of Zobah, and against the Philistines. Wherever he turned he routed them. And he did valiantly and struck the Amalekites and delivered Israel out of the hands of those who plundered them (14:47—48)."

That is not the outcome you expect based upon the earlier description of Israel's readiness for battle. It would not be surprising to read that Israel was defeated by the Philistines and became slaves, or that Israel was sacked and ruined. What is surprising is to read that Saul "routed" all of Israel's enemies—that he valiantly delivered Israel out of the hands of their enemies. If success was measured merely by the accomplishments of a man's hands, then Saul would have to be considered a dazzling success. He took Israel from certain defeat—no army, no weapons, no hope—to great victory. He was an incredibly effective military leader. Based solely on outward achievements and world-

Our accomplishments do not determine whether God considers us successful.

Success in the eyes of God is not based on your ability to impress him.

ly metrics, Saul was anything but a failure.

But our accomplishments do not determine whether God considers us successful. He is un-impressed with promotions, positions, power, and prestige. He is not enamored with trophies and titles. Success in the eyes of God is not based on your ability to impress him.

What do you view as success? What makes for a successful day? A successful year? A successful life? We need to be aware that the things we think make us a success are often based upon a false view of success. Success is not a corner office with a great view. Success is not a picture perfect family postcard, where every child is sitting still, smiling at the camera, hair neatly combed. Success is not an immaculate house that wows every visitor. Success is not moving up the corporate ladder or keeping up with our neighbors. What does it look like when you picture success? When you sink into the couch, sigh deeply, and say, "That's a successful day," what does that mean? God is not concerned with your ability to accomplish your entire to-do list. God is not impressed with your business' bottom line. God is not amazed at your ability to elicit compliments. His favor is not earned by your abilities or accomplishments. His approval is not merited by your actions or achievements. If Saul's victories were unable to impress God, then neither will yours.

How does God define success? Success is not measured by the accomplishments of your hand but by the attitude of your heart. Neither Saul's effort not his ability were the issue. The issue was his heart. Saul's heart was not wholly committed to serving God. It became painfully clear that Saul was a man after Saul's heart. His life is contrasted with the next king, David, who was a man after God's heart.

Twice in chapter 12 Samuel told the people that they could receive God's blessing if they would only fear the Lord and serve him faithfully with all their heart; if both they and their king would follow God with their whole heart and not rebel against his commands. Saul revealed a heart that was not wholly committed to God. Nowhere is Saul's sinful heart exposed more clearly than through his actions in chapters 13—14. In spite of his great military success, he failed to listen to God by offering an impatient sacrifice and making an impudent vow. In tomorrow's chapter, we will see Saul's terrible spiritual failure in the midst of his astounding military success.

Success is not measured by the accomplishments of your hand but by the attitude of your heart.

Food for Thought

The American dream of success relies heavily on self-sufficiency and self-determination. The successful person needs no one else and is beholden to no one else. They are self-made and self-reliant. Jesus speaks about this kind of self-made man and calls him a "fool (Lk 12:13—21)." An unthinking embrace of this common picture of success puts you at odds with the teaching of Jesus.

Faith in Action

Make a list of people who you think are successful and examine what they all have in common. What does your list reveal about what you think it means to be successful? Is your list heavier on accomplishments or attitudes? Read Philippians 3:3—11 and evaluate your list against Paul's testimony. Are you defining success in the same way he did?

Prayer

In your prayer time today, be honest with God about your view of success. Confess where your view does not match his and ask him for wisdom to view success from his perspective. End your time committing to him the outcome of each event on your day's schedule.

The Problem with Success Part2

1 Samuel 13–14

In 1999, movie star Brad Pitt sat down for an interview with *Rolling Stone*. At the time, he was sharing reflections on his lead role in the movie *Fight Club,* which is about a man who has the American dream and yet remains unsatisfied. Pitt provides a fascinating look into how people view success. He told the interviewer, "Man, I know all these things are supposed to seem important to us—the car, the condo, our version of success—but if that's the case, why is the general feeling out there reflecting more impotence and isolation and desperation and loneliness? If you ask me, I say toss all this—we gotta find something else. Because all I know is that at this point in time, we are heading for a dead end, a numbing of the soul, a complete atrophy of the spiritual being. And I do not want that (*Rolling Stone,* 10/28/1999)."

Saul was not a man after God's heart.

People view Brad Pitt as a success. He is wealthy, handsome, famous, and influential. His accomplishments are impressive. But he understood that success could not be achieved by more accomplishments. He was beginning to learn the lesson God taught King Saul. Saul had impressive military success, but he was a failure because of the attitude of his heart. His heart condition was revealed in a both a foolish sacrifice and a foolish vow.

While the Philistines were amassing for battle, Saul was stuck waiting for the prophet Samuel to arrive to offer a sacrifice to God. Sick of waiting, Saul decided to offer the sacrifice himself (vv. 8—9). As soon as he was finished, Samuel arrived and condemned his sin (vv. 10—12). Because of his disobedience, the dynasty was removed from Saul's family (vv. 13—14). His impatient sacrifice violated the command he was given by Samuel. But the issue was deeper than the sacrifice. The real issue, revealed by the sacrifice, was that Saul was not a man after God's heart. Samuel's message to him was that he would be replaced, not by his son, but by another man who, in contrast to Saul, would be a man after God's heart.

Notice what Saul's actions revealed about his heart. He certainly understood the command from Samuel. Not only did he know exactly what Samuel meant when he asked, "What have you done (v. 11)?" but also he told Samuel that he "forced" himself to offer the sacrifice (v. 12). Saul was not ignorant about what the command entailed or how he was breaking the command when he offered the sacrifice. If he knew he was breaking God's command, why did he do it? He had a three-fold problem: the people were deserting him, Samuel had not arrived, and the Philistines were preparing to attack (v. 11). Saul's dilemma was real. It would be unfair to assume Saul took the command lightly and disobeyed without any reservation. The enemy was bearing down and his army was dwindling, yet he still waited seven days for Samuel to arrive. Saul was not a flagrant rebel, callously disregarding the commands of God. He was trying to wait. He was doing his best, but he reached a point where he decided that he had no other option but to disobey God. When push came to shove, Saul was unwilling to trust God. Somewhere in the midst of his waiting, he had determined that God's command was not ultimate, and he had the authority to disregard it if necessary.

Moses gave instructions to future kings of Israel to make a copy of God's law, read it regularly, and keep it (Deut 17:18–20). According to Moses, a king after God's own heart, wholly committed to what God is committed to, will keep all the words of God's law and not turn aside to the right hand or to the left. Saul's sin was more than impatience; it was unbelief. It was rooted in a belief that every word of God's could not be trusted. It was reserving the right to turn left or right if God did not come through.

Saul's heart was revealed when he made an impatient sacrifice and also when he made an imprudent vow. Remember the desperate situation Israel found itself in. The vast and well-equipped Philistine army was advancing. Things looked bleak. In that moment, Saul's son Jonathan devised a plan. He and his armor-bearer decided to approach the Philistine garrison on the other side of a rocky crag (14:1–5). Jonathan's

Nothing of lasting value can be accomplished apart from God's divine intervention.

> *Success is not found in autonomy, but in allegiance*

secret plan was bold and risky. But he was confident it would succeed because he asked God to show them whether or not they would be victorious (vv. 6—11). God gave them a sign, and so they attacked, killing twenty men and securing the garrison (vv. 12—15). Jonathan was not confident because of his own strength. His confidence was not in his cunning. His confidence was in God. He said, "It may be that the LORD will work for us, for nothing can hinder the LORD from saving by many or by few (v. 7)." Unlike his father, Jonathan did not default to his own strength. God gave Jonathan strength to defeat the Philistines.

Saul decided to attack before Jonathan returned to camp from his victory (vv. 16—23). God showed again that he could be trusted. He caused Israel to be successful. It was his strength that vanquished the enemy. Nothing of lasting value can be accomplished apart from God's divine intervention. It was at this point that Saul made another foolish decision. Despite the army's fatigue, he imprudently leveled a curse against anyone who ate anything before he was avenged against his enemies (v. 24). As they chased the army, they entered a forest and saw honey lying on the ground. Because they feared Saul's vow, the soldiers did not eat the honey. Jonathan had not heard about the vow, so when he saw the honey, he stopped, ate it, and was refreshed (v. 27). After he ate, one of the soldiers told Jonathan about Saul's vow, and Jonathan saw the foolishness of what Saul had done. The food would have energized the army and brought a greater victory (vv. 29—30).

After the victory, the people slaughtered animals and ate them raw, a violation of the law God had given them (vv. 31—32). Saul brought the people together and commanded them to offer sacrifices to God for their sin (vv. 33—35). Saul's action in building the altar to sacrifice for the people was noble, but we cannot forget what led them into their sin. The cause of their sinful actions was the hunger brought on by Saul's foolish vow. Saul was being revealed as a king who was not leading his people to follow the Lord, but a king whose actions misled the people.

When Saul found out Jonathan had eaten the honey, he decided Jonathan would have to die (vv. 36—44). The people rose up against his decision because they understood he was innocent (v. 45). The problem was not his taste of honey; it was Saul's poor leadership. Jonathan did not deserve to die. He had been used by God to accomplish a great victory. This entire episode clearly demonstrated that Saul was not a man after God's own heart. Saul was not wholly committed to God's ways and purposes. A man after God's own heart does not kill the man whom God raised up to deliver his people.

What can we learn from this sad account of Saul's failure? We learn that success does not come through our effort, cannot be measured in titles or possessions, and will not be gained by earning trophies or winning battles. Success is not found in climbing the ladder but in bending the knee. It is not found in autonomy, but in allegiance. It is not found in self-sufficiency but in submission. Success is serving the Lord with all of our heart, being wholly committed to God's ways and purposes. How successful are you in God's eyes? Pursue

Success is serving the Lord with all of our heart, being wholly committed to God's ways and purposes.

godly success, not through your effort, but through total and complete submission.

Food for Thought Genuine faith does not leave a loophole. It does not figure a way out or craft an escape plan. Genuine faith says to God, "You alone bring salvation. There is nothing I can do on my own." King Saul was willing to partially trust God to save him, but he left the door open to return to his own effort. Faith is following God's command regardless of the circumstances. Are you trusting God with your whole heart? Or have you left an escape hatch?

Faith in Action

Success is measured by total and complete submission to God. It can be difficult to submit to God when he does not answer your prayers on your timetable. Are there certain requests you are praying for that God has not answered? Are you tempted to take them in your own hands and figure out your own solution? Submission means trusting God even when he has not answered in the way you think he should have.

Prayer

What sin do you need God to rescue you from today? Pray about it. The same God who delivered the Philistine garrison into Jonathan's hands ,and delivered you from death and hell, can deliver you from that sin which seems to dominate you.

The Danger of Disobedience

1 Samuel 15

There is a phrase, only five words long, that is almost always untrue. Sometimes we say it to others when we do not really mean it, and sometimes we use it to convince ourselves. Whenever we say the phrase—"It's not a big deal"—it is certainly a big deal. When someone spills grape soda on your new carpet, and you say, "It's not a big deal," it's a lie. It's what you say instead of throwing a tantrum, which is what you really want to do.

The most dangerous way we use the phrase—"it's not a big deal"—is when we say it to ourselves in an attempt to justify something we know we shouldn't do. Whenever you hear that voice inside your head whisper, "It's not a big deal," you should know it's a lie. If something is really not a big deal, we do not need to convince ourselves it's not a big deal. What that internal voice is really telling us is this, "Disobedience is not dangerous. Do not worry about the consequences. You'll be fine." This account in Saul's life is a sober warning about the consequences of disobeying God. Disobedience is dangerous.

> *Disobedience is dangerous.*

A few years ago, I read a biography of Abraham Lincoln. When I told my wife that I finally finished it, she jokingly asked, "How did it end?" As I read the story of Lincoln, I knew what was coming. I knew Lincoln's life ended with an assassin's bullet. The weeks and months leading up to that event dwell in its shadow. Day blends with day as events spiral toward the bitter and painful end. Reading 1 Samuel feels like reading the last few chapters of Lincoln's biography. As a reader, I know how Saul's story is going to end. I know what is coming. I know his life will end with a soldier's arrow. Each event is another downward step that ends with his bitter and painful death.

After Israel's repentance and restoration in chapter seven, they begged Samuel for a king. Even though the Israelites had a king (the King of all the earth), they longed to be like the unbelieving nations around them. God answered their request by giving them a king like all the other nations. He gave them a king who was tall and impressive, and then God gave him a great victory in chapter 11. But the downward steps begin in chapter 13, when Saul decided to rebel against God's command and offered a sacrifice instead of waiting for Samuel. That action—and the heart behind it—caused Saul's family to lose the chance for a dynasty. Because of his sin, his sons would not succeed him as king. Chapter 15 recounts the next downward step, as Saul once again rebelled against God's command. This time the kingdom was torn not simply from his family, but also from him.

This chapter revolves around Saul's disobedience— five different times Saul's sin is mentioned (vv. 11, 19, 23,

24, 26). Saul's sin of disobedience is described as turning away from following God, not carrying out God's instructions, not obeying God's voice, doing evil in God's sight, rejecting God's word, and transgressing God's commands. Using clear, vivid, and descriptive language, Samuel indicted Saul on a charge of disobedience, and it was a big deal.

Saul needed to hear about his numerous and varied sins because he thought he was obedient (vv.13, 20). There was a serious misunderstanding between Samuel and Saul, and more importantly between God and Saul. Saul, the disobedient king, claimed to obey God. The author of this account uses Saul's actions to help us understand what disobedience looks like and how dangerous it is. Disobedience really is a big deal.

Saul's actions reveal three different ways we disobey God. First, disobedience happens when you reject God's authority. The very first verse of this chapter sets the context for Saul's disobedience. Saul was anointed king (v. 1), which means he was not the ultimate authority. God chose Saul to be king over Israel—the anointing was the sign of God's choice. God set Saul aside for His use. Not only did God choose Saul, but God also chose Samuel to anoint him as king. Samuel, by virtue of the role God had given him as prophet, spoke on God's behalf. Saul needed to listen to Samuel because Samuel spoke the words of the Lord.

The words of the Lord from Samuel to Saul were clear. Saul was to lead the people to utterly destroy the Amalekites (v. 3), not leaving a single person or animal alive. The army of Saul would serve as God's judgment on Amalek for their sin against his people, which

Disobedience happens when you reject God's authority.

> *Each sin, whether great or small, is a power struggle between you and God.*

is recorded in Exodus 17. Saul did not obey the command. He made a decision to spare Agag, the king of the Amalekites, and the best of the sheep and oxen (v. 9).

When Samuel confronted ed Saul about his sin, he again reminded Saul of God's choice of Saul as king (v. 17). He basically asked Saul, "Did not God appoint you as leader of the people?" This question served two purposes. First, it did not allow Saul to blame the people, even though he attempted to do so. Second, it reminded him that God was the one in charge. God is the ultimate authority. Every time you disobey God, you are rejecting his authority over your life. Each sin, whether great or small, is a power struggle between you and God.

Second, disobedience happens when you revise God's commands. When Saul responded to Samuel he revised God's command (v. 15). When did God mention anything about sparing sheep for sacrifice? Saul did the same thing again in verse 20. Both times Saul revised the command of God to better suit himself. We all have the tendency to do this. We read a command of God's, and we start editing. We pull out our red pen and modify that command until it says something more comfortable. How many times have you read a verse and said, "What Jesus really means is..." If we are honest, we might describe our Bible study in the following way: read, then redefine; read, then rationalize; read, then revise. Do you see the arrogance displayed in Saul's revision? When he decided to revise God's command and spare the

> *Disobedience happens when you revise God's commands.*

animals, he was saying in essence, "God, you do not know what's best." "God, your way will not work." "God, I know better."

Disobedience happens when you replace God's opinion.

Third, disobedience happens when you replace God's opinion. A theme that runs through this passage was Saul's concern

about what the people said about him. Saul was more concerned about the people's opinion of him than about God's opinion (vv. 15, 21). There appeared to be little concern on his part about what God said. Saul did not fear the judgment of God. Like the moon eclipsing the sun, God's opinion had been eclipsed by Saul's fear of the people.

Saul focused on maintaining his reputation with the people, and as a result, he ignored his relationship with God. Never trade your relationship with God for an improved reputation with people. That is like trading a private plane for a broken scooter. Saul's concern was his own reputation, which is why when Samuel arrived he discovered Saul had just set up a monument to himself (v. 12). It appears the reason Saul spared Agag was so he would have a trophy of his conquest. Even after Samuel declared God's judgment on Saul, Saul was still more concerned about the people's judgment of him (v. 30). How sad. How foolish to be more concerned about people's opinion of you than you are about God's opinion. What are you more concerned about? Do you lose sleep over what people say about you? Do you fear what someone can do to you? Are you anxious about someone's power to impact your life? God's judgment is the only judgment that matters.

Food for Thought There are times your sin is fueled by ignorance, but your sin is always born out of a rebellious heart. It is rooted in a desire for control. You want to be in charge of your own life. Like Eve in the Garden and Saul with the Amalekites, you want to be able to choose for yourself what is right and wrong. You will not see victory over sin until you settle the issue of authority. Who has authority over your life? Will you pursue God's will or default to your own?

Faith in Action Just like individual Christians, churches need to guard against the arrogance that says we know better how to do church than God does. Our guide for faith and practice must never be the Wall Street Journal. We are not dependent on the latest Lifeway publication. God does not call us to be creative, but obedient. And obedience means following his commands without revision, no matter how radical they seem. Write a note today encouraging your pastor to stay faithful to God's Word.

Prayer

Life is made up of a few major decisions and a million mundane ones, and God owns them all—every single one. Pray that God will empower you to bring every area of your life under his authority. Ask him for wisdom to see if there are areas in your life that you have not turned over to his authority.

Whole-Hearted Submission

1 Samuel 15:22—23

From Saul's sin we learn that disobedience happens when we reject God's authority, revise God's commands, or replace God's judgment. What about obedience? What does obedience look like? If we take the charges against Saul and flip them, obedience is following God, performing God's commandments, obeying God's voice, doing right in God's sight, accepting God's word, and abiding by God's commands.

Samuel helps us understand obedience even more when he confronted Saul about his disobedience to God's command. He said, "Has the LORD as great delight in burnt offerings and sacrifices, as in obeying the voice of the LORD? Behold, to obey is better than sacrifice, and to listen than the fat of rams. For rebellion is as the sin of divination, and presumption is as iniquity and idolatry. Because you have rejected the word of the LORD, he has also rejected you from being king (vv. 22—23)." Samuel's point was that obedience is more than outward conformity. Obedience is a heart wholly submitted to God.

Obedience is more than conformity to a set of external rituals. That was Samuel's point. Obedience cannot be reduced to compliance. Obedience must flow from a heart wholly submitted to God. It is not enough to throw a sheep on an altar or sacrifice a bull. That can be done with a heart hardened to the Word of God. It was a tendency of the Israelites—and it is our tendency as well—to make external performance synonymous with obedience.

Echoing Samuel's words, later prophets repeatedly warned Israel about the danger of moral conformity without a heart of obedience. Hosea said, "For I desire steadfast love and not sacrifice, the knowledge of God rather than burnt offerings (6:6)." Jeremiah quoted God to the people, "For in the day that I brought them out of the land of Egypt, I did not speak to your fathers or command them concerning burnt offerings and sacrifices. But this command I gave them: 'Obey my voice, and I will be your God, and you shall be my people. And walk in all the way that I command you, that it may be well with you (7:22—23).'"

Jesus reiterated this same point in the Gospel of Mark. One of the lawyers of the day, a scribe, asked him which commandment was the most important. Jesus quoted Deuteronomy six and said it was to love the Lord with all your heart, soul, mind, and strength. The second great commandment is to love your neighbor as yourself. The scribe responded, "You are right, Teacher. You have truly said that he is one, and there is no other besides him. And to love him with all the heart and with all the understanding and with all the strength, and to love one's neighbor as oneself, is much more than all whole burnt offerings and sacrifices (Mark 12:32—33)." Jesus told him he answered wisely and was close to receiving salvation. In essence Jesus was saying, "Yes, you get it. Rituals and ceremonies without a heart of submission are meaningless. The obedience God desires begins in the heart."

Our human tendency will always be to default to externalism. Instead of submitting wholeheartedly to God, we will compartmentalize obedience. We will turn obedience into external conformity. We will reject God's authority in our hearts while making sacrifice with our hands. We will revise God's commands while leading our bull to the altar. The reason we drift toward externalism is because we can do it on our own. We can handle performance-based external conformity ourselves. It does not require us to ask for help. Externalism is salvation without God. It is salvation where I get to be my own god.

Externalism requires you to conform, but obedience requires you to be transformed. The draw of externalism is that you have enough power to conform yourself on the outside, but you will never have enough power to transform yourself on the inside. Many professing Christians have turned obedience to God into a checklist. They make a list of things they should not do like, "Do not watch bad movies. Do not say certain words. Do not drink alcohol. Do not...do not...do not." Next they make a list of things they have to do like, "Do read my Bible. Do go to church. Do give 10%. Do...do...do." A checklist of do's and don'ts misses the whole point. The obedience God demands requires his help. Do you need help to obey God? Could you make it through the day obeying him on your own? What did you need his help to do this past week?

Externalism requires you to conform, but obedience requires you to be transformed.

> *If your version of obedience can be accomplished without God's help, then your version of obedience does not match God's.*

If your version of obedience can be accomplished without God's help, then your version of obedience does not match God's.

Obedience—wholehearted submission to God—requires outside help because it requires internal change. Obedience requires a new heart, and only God can do that. This is the miracle of the new covenant. God said: "But this is the covenant that I will make with the house of Israel after those days, declares the LORD: I will put my law within them, and I will write it on their hearts. And I will be their God, and they shall be my people (Jer 31:33)." Jesus shed his blood on the cross to inaugurate this new covenant. His death was necessary for you to be given a new heart—a heart that could obey God. Have you received this new covenant? Have you trusted in Jesus' work for your salvation or are you relating to God on the basis of your works?

Just as the sun always sets to the west, you, like King Saul before you, will always drift toward externalism. It is easier. It is manageable. Externalism exchanges the impossible for the possible, the unachievable for the achievable, the unreachable for the reachable, and the unattainable for the attainable. Externalism cuts God out and makes you supreme. You need to be vigilant to ground your obedience in God's grace.

If your heart has been changed it will be revealed by what you do. A heart wholly submitted to God is revealed in external obedience. Samuel was not condemning sacrifice and burnt offering, just like we would not condemn

> *Obedience—wholehearted submission to God—requires outside help because it requires internal change.*

church attendance and giving. Samuel was saying sacrifice and burnt offering without a submitted heart has no more value than grilling a steak.

Food for Thought Years after this account, King David, who unlike Saul was committed to God with his whole heart, wrote, "The sacrifices of God are a broken spirit; a broken and contrite heart, O God, you will not despise (Ps 51:17)." God does not want your sheep; he wants you. He does not need your money; he desires your heart. Does he have it?

Faith in Action

If you are a parent, consider how you discipline your children. Is your goal for them to be conformed or transformed? Are you prayerfully dealing with their heart or simply dealing with their actions? Do not confuse compliance with submission. Do not teach your children that conformity equals obedience.

Prayer

Pastors are susceptible to preaching a gospel of performance and setting up external standards as the measure of spirituality. They need to reject any extra-biblical requirements that give the appearance of obedience. Pray for your pastors and elders. Pray that the gospel of grace—the gospel that transforms—will be their consistent message.

Eyes of Faith

1 Samuel 16:1–13

I am basically blind. Without glasses or contacts, I can barely see. To read anything, I have to hold it right next to my nose. When I wake up, everything is fuzzy and out of focus. But when the glasses go on, or the contacts go in, everything changes. These two drastically different ways of seeing the world affect everything I do. If you have bad eyesight, imagine what it would be like to go through a day without corrective lenses. The world would be exactly the same, but your understanding of it and interaction with it would change completely.

Spiritually we are all born with defective eyesight. We do not see the world or interact with the world in the way God intended. What should be clear to us is instead fuzzy and indistinct. Nowhere is this more clear in the Bible than the book of Judges, which is the time preceding the accounts of 1 Samuel. In the book of Judges, we find a certain description repeated over and over: "The people did what was right in their own eyes." The people, with faulty vision, attempted to determine what was best for them to do. Blinded by sin, they stumbled through life creating havoc all around them. This low point in Israel's

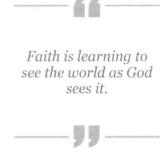

Faith is learning to see the world as God sees it.

history was due to faulty spiritual eyesight. When the book of Samuel begins, Eli, a blind priest, was leading Israel in worship. A blind man was leading a nation of blind men. Every man was trying to do what looked best to him, but no one could see.

Today's passage shows us a different way to view the world. While there is only one world, there are two ways of viewing it. One is through eyes clouded by sin and unbelief. The other is through eyes of faith. By faith we can see the world as God sees it. God sees the world and all that is in it perfectly. Nothing is fuzzy or out of focus for him. By faith we can begin to see with clarity what would otherwise be foreign to us. Faith is glasses for the spiritually blind, changing both how we see and engage with the world we live in.

The Hebrew word for "see" is used seven times in this chapter (vv. 1, 6, 7, 17, 18), contrasting the way God sees with the way humans see. Our eyes deceive us; they do not show us what is truly going on in the world. The essence of faith is seeing beyond what our eyes can see (Heb 11:1—3). Faith is seeing what is unseen—it is confidence that what is not visible created and governs that which is visible. Faith is learning to see the world as God sees it. In this passage, we discover two contrasting ways of looking at the world: one way is with human eyes and the other is with eyes of faith. It is hard not to be blinded by our circumstances. Like fish in water, we swim in the sea of our circumstances every day. We cannot avoid our circumstances—they are the situations of life. Sometimes the circumstances are good, and sometimes they are bad.

But both good and bad circumstances can fill our vision and obstruct our view of anything else.

The chapter opens after God had torn Saul's kingdom from him and his descendants. Samuel was mourning the coming end of Saul's reign when God said to him, "How long are you going to keep mourning for Saul? I am the one who rejected him as king (v. 1)." Samuel was in the fog of disappointment, and he could not see more than a few feet. He was depressed over what happened with Saul. Everything had gone wrong. In his disappointment he failed to trust God to act. But God was going to act. God said, "I have selected a king from the sons of Jesse (v. 1)." The word "selected" is actually the word "seen." While all Samuel could see was his disappointment, God had seen a king whom he would anoint. God was still working. His plans were coming to pass.

Beware the power of disappointment and disillusionment. Eyes of faith are necessary to see beyond disappointment and trust that God is still working. His plans will still come to pass, and his king will still reign. Samuel had to stop mourning Saul and focus on anointing the next king, the one whose line would produce the Messiah.

Samuel was not only blinded by disappointing circumstances but also by fearful circumstances (v. 2). His fear was legitimate; Saul was a powerful warrior who controlled the army. If he were to hear that Samuel was anointing a new king, he would most likely respond with vengeance. Samuel was like many in the Bible who struggled with fear. Moses was afraid to head back to Egypt to rescue God's people. Jeremiah was afraid to take on the role of prophet. The disciples were afraid

Eyes of faith are necessary to see beyond disappointment and trust that God is still working.

> *The Bible is filled with God's promises to walk with us in times when we're afraid.*

to head to Jerusalem because of the religious leaders. The Bible is filled with examples of men and women responding with fear to the commands of God. Their circumstances loomed so large in their eyes, they shook with fear. But the Bible is filled with God's promises to walk with us in times when we're afraid. Eyes of faith see the hand of God, guiding and protecting us, even in the most fearful circumstances. Eyes of faith see the good shepherd, whose rod and staff comfort us, even in the valley of the shadow of death. We need to lift our eyes from our circumstances, and place them on King Jesus.

When Samuel arrived in Bethlehem to anoint one of Jesse's sons as the next king, he saw Eliab, the oldest son, and assumed he would become king (v. 6). Why did Samuel think Eliab was the going to be the next king? Because Eliab looked like a king. In fact, he probably reminded Samuel of Saul, whose defining characteristic was his stature (9:2). Eliab, like Saul, had the appearance of a king—tall and impressive. But appearance isn't everything. In fact, God is not impressed by outward appearance. God's view is not limited like ours is—he sees both outside and inside (v. 7).

Years ago, I went to a professional basketball game. Instead of buying tickets ahead of time we decided to buy some from a scalper outside the stadium. The only cheap seats we could find were "obstructed view" seats—there was a roof support pillar between us and the court. Similarly, we live with an obstructed view. We cannot see what is really going on inside a person's heart. All we see is the outside. We see appearances, not affections. We see what they want us to see, not what they really think. God's view is unobstructed. He sees the whole person. He sees what they really think, what they really desire, and what they really love. In a world where so much is judged by appearance, God does not judge that way. God did not care how tall or attractive Eliab was. He only cared about the condition of Eliab's heart. He told Samuel earlier that he would select a king "after his own heart (13:14)." God wanted a king who loved the very same things he loved.

The fact that God sees our hearts, and what we really love, is both terrifying and life-giving. It is terrifying because our hearts love all the wrong things, but it is life-giving because God has made a way for our hearts to be made new. God sees every dark corner of your heart, including the things you would never admit to anyone else. He sees the most shameful, secret thoughts you have ever had. Do you really think he will overlook any sin? No. But, Jesus died so that every sinful streak in your heart could be scrubbed clean. Jesus makes hearts new. When God looks at your heart, does he see your old, sin-stained heart, or does he see a new one, washed clean by the blood of Jesus?

Samuel saw the seven oldest sons of Jesse and assumed each tall, strong son would be chosen as king. But God chose none of them. After seeing them he asked Jesse, "Are there any others (v. 11) ?" "There is still the youngest," he answered, "but right now he is tending the sheep." Samuel told Jesse, "Send for him. We will not sit down to eat until he gets here." When he arrived, God told Samuel to anoint him. God chose the unlikely one, just as he had so often in Scripture, and his choice of the unlikely son to be king assures us that we do not have to measure up to some outward standard in order to be

Jesus died so that every sinful streak in your heart could be scrubbed clean.

loved by him. God sees affections, not appearances. With eyes of faith, we too can learn to see what really matters.

Food for Thought *We so often judge others based upon appearances. Racism is judging people based upon their skin color. When Martin Luther King, Jr. said, "I have a dream that my four little children will one day live in a nation where they will not be judged by the color of their skin, but by the content of their character," he was echoing this passage. God does not judge based on appearances, like skin color, but by the content of the heart. We need eyes of faith to see what matters most to God and then act accordingly.*

Faith helps us worry less about how we *Faith in Action* *appear to others, and instead focus on the condition of our heart. It is easy to wonder what others think about us and how we appear to them, rather than being concerned about what is going on inside our hearts. Faith frees us from the powerful pull of impressing people so that we can focus instead on loving people. Since God looks past appearances and focuses on affections, faith helps you to focus your attention on what really matters—the condition of your heart. What condition is your heart in today?*

Prayer

Do you live in fear? It could be fear of sickness, fear of rejection, fear of exhaustion, or fear of harm. If you are a Christian, you belong to Jesus, who conquered death and hell and given you his Spirit, not to live in fear but to live in faith. Read Romans 8:31—39 and ask God to help you live by faith, not in fear.

A Picture of Jesus

1 Samuel 16:14–23

How do we develop eyes of faith? The author of Hebrews describes faith and then illustrates it with person after person who learned to see beyond their circumstances and past outward appearances (ch. 11). He then gives us a command: "Therefore, since we are surrounded by so great a cloud of witnesses, let us also lay aside every weight, and sin which clings so closely, and let us run with endurance the race that is set before us, Looking to Jesus, the founder and perfecter of our faith, who for the joy that was set before him endured the cross, despising the shame, and is seated at the right hand of the throne of God (Heb 12:1–2)." We develop eyes of faith by placing our eyes on Jesus. If we want to see beyond our circumstances and past appearances, we must look above them to Jesus. Seeing Jesus, focusing our attention and affection on him, and creates and nourishes a life of faith.

In the end of chapter 16 we find a beautiful picture of the coming Messiah. In David, we get a glimpse of Jesus, and focusing on him will help us learn to see life more and more as God does. Three descriptions of David point us to Jesus. First, he is a shepherd who guides the

We develop eyes of faith by placing our eyes on Jesus.

flock. Where was David when all the other brothers were paraded before Samuel? He was out in the field tending the flock (v. 11). The description of the Messiah as a loving shepherd is prominent throughout Scripture. God himself is described as a shepherd who meets all of our needs and guards us in his presence forever. David, the shepherd king, was placed over Israel to guide them, lead them, and protect them from enemies. His care becomes a picture of the care the Messiah will show for all God's people (Ezek. 34:23). Unlike the religious leaders who neglected and even harmed the sheep, Jesus loves and protects his sheep.

Does your faith need to grow? Ponder the wonder that Jesus is your shepherd. Look to him as the only one who knows how to navigate through this life. When he calls, trust his voice, even if many other voices call for your attention. The heart of faith is trusting what Jesus says even if it does not make sense in your eyes. If you are in a situation right now where Jesus says to do one thing, but your heart, your intuition, and your gut is telling you to do another, look to Jesus. Eyes of faith see Jesus walking before you, and seeing him helps you trust him when the path has mountains looming on both sides.

The coming Messiah is not only a shepherd who guides his flock, but he is also a warrior who defeats his enemies. After David was anointed as king, the scene shifts to King Saul's courtroom, where Saul was being tormented by an evil spirit. This was not necessarily a demon, but a messenger of misery sent by God as judgment upon Saul's sin. Saul was looking for relief when one of his servants suggested finding someone to come and play music to soothe him. He commanded them to find a musician. One of Saul's servants suggested David, because he was not only a talented musician, but because he was also a brave warrior and the Lord was with him (v. 18).

David was described as a warrior, and in the very next chapter we learn why. He killed the giant Goliath and led Israel to the first of many victories. The Messiah, like David before him, is a great warrior who defeats the enemies of God's people. He defeats the giants of death and hell. Do you need to trust Jesus and not fear? Look to the warrior king who rose triumphant from the dead and now sits at the right hand of the Father. When you feel like Samuel, threatened by violence, and this threat blocks your vision, look beyond it to Jesus, who crushed the Serpent's head and rendered all enemies toothless.

The coming Messiah is a shepherd, a warrior, and a servant filled with the Spirit. When David was anointed, the Spirit of the Lord came upon him in a powerful way from that point forward (v. 13). In the past, the Spirit of God had come upon leaders, like Samson, Gideon, and Saul, but only at certain times. The Spirit would usually come upon a leader to help him win a battle or make a prophecy. After the event, the Spirit of the Lord would depart. David was different: the Spirit of the Lord came upon him more permanently, and by the Spirit's power, he was able to serve Saul by playing skillfully and driving the messenger of misery away from the king (v. 23).

David was a partial picture of the coming Messiah, whom the prophet Isaiah described this way: "There shall come forth a shoot from the stump of Jesse, and a branch from his roots shall bear

Jesus loves and protects his sheep.

fruit. And the Spirit of the LORD shall rest upon him, the Spirit of wisdom and understanding, the Spirit of counsel and might, the Spirit of knowledge and the fear of the LORD (11:1–2)." When Jesus began His public ministry he was baptized by John the Baptist, and the Spirit of the Lord descended on him like a dove. Throughout his ministry, he served in the power of the Spirit.

> *Eyes of faith see Jesus walking before you, and seeing him helps you trust him when the path has mountains looming on both sides.*

Before Jesus ascended to heaven, he promised to send his Spirit to permanently indwell his followers. The same Spirit who empowered David's victories and rested on Jesus during his ministry, now lives inside each believer. If you are a Christian, you have the Spirit inside you, and the Spirit dwelling in you can produce eyes of faith to see Jesus reigning over and above your circumstances.

I remember my wife's grandmother telling us the story about the day she put on her glasses and started going about her daily routine. But something was not right. Everything was a bit off, and partway through the day she started to get a headache. At the same time, she got a call from her husband asking her if she had seen his glasses at the house before she left. Not feeling well, she gave a short answer and hung up the phone. When she finally got home and greeted her husband, her looked at her and said, "Why are you wearing my glasses?"

Is that you? Something is definitely wrong—you are frustrated, you cannot see well, and you are getting a headache. You can go through life with blurred vision, focused on depressing and fearful circumstances, and how people appear to you. Or, you can see with eyes of faith, focused on the shepherd who is guiding you, the warrior who fights your battles, and the servant whose Spirit lives within you. How do you see the world? Are you looking with eyes of faith? If not, look to Jesus. You develop eyes of faith by putting your eyes on him.

If you are a Christian, you have the Spirit inside you, and the Spirit dwelling in you can produce eyes of faith to see Jesus reigning over and above your circumstances.

Food for Thought

After his resurrection from the dead, Jesus showed the disciples how the Law of Moses, the Prophets, and the Psalms all wrote about him (Lk 24:44). Are you looking for Jesus when you read the Old Testament? To read the Old Testament without seeing Jesus misses the point and leads to legalism (Jn 5:39).

Faith in Action

Learn to see Jesus in the Old Testament. Read Acts 2:14—41 and notice the different ways Peter points to Jesus from the Old Testament. The apostle Paul similarly points to Jesus from the Old Testament when giving his defense before King Agrippa in Acts 26. How can you follow their example of seeing how all of Scripture points to Jesus?

Prayer

Pray that God would help you see clearly how the Scriptures point to Jesus. Seeing Jesus is what brings life transformation—we become like him as we behold him in his Word (2 Cor 3:18). Ask God to help you behold Jesus and become more like him.

The Real Champion

1 Samuel 17

I remember watching a boxing movie when I was young and hearing a biblical allusion—an allusion which is common in both sports movies and actual sporting competitions. One of the commentators in the movie described the upcoming boxing match as a classic battle between David and Goliath. Viewing the story of David and Goliath as the prototypical underdog story misses the point. David versus Goliath was not an underdog story, but a story about the power of God's salvation.

If you view David and Goliath as an underdog story, that means you identify with the wrong person. The story is not intended to show you how to topple the giants in your life or how to win when the odds are stacked against you. The story shows God's grace and mercy to deliver his people when they cannot deliver themselves. This classic story, told and retold for three-thousand years, has far more depth and contains far greater hope, than most people realize. Understanding it can instill courage and inspire confidence in those who follow Jesus.

The entire first half of this account is intended to teach us the lesson that some battles cannot be won by

> *Eyes of faith see Jesus walking before you, and seeing him helps you trust him when the path has mountains looming on both sides.*

human strength. There are some battles too big for us, some battles we cannot win without help. The account opens with two armies on either side of a valley. As they stared at each other from opposite sides, neither wanted to sacrifice the high ground by sending their troops into the ravine in the middle (vv. 1—3). Into the valley marched a giant.

The giant's description revealed the futility of Israel's position (vv. 4—7). He was huge. He was unbeatable. What hope did Israel possibly have to defeat him? Goliath is called a "champion"—a word that literally means "the one who is between." He stood in between the armies as a representative of the Philistine army. He would fight under the Philistine banner, and his victory would be their victory. Goliath's weapons were not only massive, they were technically advanced—made from bronze. In every way, he and his army were superior to the army of Israel. Looking at Goliath, everything seemed hopeless. But looks are deceptive. No matter how the situation appears, God determines the outcome.

Goliath issued a challenge to the army of Israel. He challenged the army to select one warrior to fight him in single, ritual combat. The winner of the contest would be the winner of the war. If he was defeated, he promised Israel that his people, the Philistines, would lay down their weapons and become their servants (vv. 8—10). But no one from Israel thought they could defeat Goliath in single combat (v. 11).

The author of 1 Samuel makes a subtle point by including Goliath's height. He is the third character in 1 Samuel described as tall. The first was King Saul, the second was David's oldest brother, Eliab, and now Goliath. All three were at the battleground, but neither the first nor the second was tall enough to face Goliath. Even though Saul and Eliab towered over other people, they ran into a warrior who towered over them. Instead of stepping out of his tent, marching down into the valley, and accepting Goliath's challenge, King Saul offered great riches and honor to anyone who would fight and kill the giant (v. 25). He would be given money, a place in the royal family, and his family would be relieved of the burden of paying taxes (vv. 24–25). No one accepted it. No one thought Goliath could be beaten. They knew this battle was too big for them to fight. This battle could not be won by human strength.

The second major lesson of the account of David and Goliath is that God's champion won the unwinnable battle. David won. He defeated Goliath, doing what King Saul and all of Saul's mighty warriors could not. The unwinnable battle was won by the champion God chose. Notice three important observations about God's chosen champion

First, God's champion was an unlikely man who won in an unexpected way. Verse 17 cuts away from the scene of Goliath's taunting of the army of Israel, and focuses on David, who had returned to his familiar role of caring for the sheep. While the armies of Israel were amassed to stop the Philistines, David was at home helping with chores. His father gave him a new chore. He was to take food to his brothers who were part of Saul's army. As he loaded the food to take it to his brothers, no one thought this young shepherd boy would be the one to defeat the mighty giant. No one would have imagined that he

> *Eyes of faith see Jesus walking before you, and seeing him helps you trust him when the path has mountains looming on both sides.*

> *David versus Goliath was not an underdog story, but a story about the power of God's salvation.*

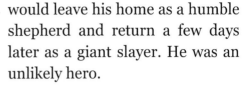

would leave his home as a humble shepherd and return a few days later as a giant slayer. He was an unlikely hero.

Not even his brothers thought David was special. When David heard Goliath taunt the army, he responded with frustration at Goliath's blasphemy and the army's inactivity. David's own brothers mocked him and falsely accused him. They claimed to know his heart was filled with arrogance and evil, even though we know David had a heart filled with love for God (v. 29).

The way David won was by rejecting the armor of Saul—the normal choice for single combat—in favor of his slingshot and five smooth stones from the creek bed. David won the battle against the giant in a way that mystified the expectations of those watching. David became Israel's champion. He was the one "who steps between." He was the representative for God's people, and his victory became their victory. His defeat of Goliath did not just win the battle for himself, but for all the people of God.

Second, God's champion was passionate about God's people and zealous for God's reputation. David viewed Goliath as an animal attacking God's flock (vv. 34—37). Goliath was a predator stalking the flock of God's people, and David, the shepherd, was not going to let him feast on the sheep. As strong as David's love for the people was, what really stood out was his zeal for God's reputation (vv. 26, 36, 45—47). He was motivated by the reputation of his God. How dare someone mock and defy the one true God—David could not bear to hear it.

He twice referred to God as "the living God." Unlike the gods of the Philistines which were nothing more than fictional identities attached to carved stones, David's God was alive. When David stood facing Goliath, he was confident in the battle's outcome for one reason. He knew that God's glory would spread far and wide through the giant's defeat (v. 46). This was an opportunity for the whole world to hear about the one true and living God.

Third, God's champion was the head-crushing Savior promised at the very beginning. Everything that took place that day in the Valley of Elah points to the Messiah and the victory God promised in the Garden of Eden. When Adam and Eve sinned, they lost everything. But in that moment God made a promise, and the rest of the Bible unfolds the promise. God promised a champion who would save humanity by crushing the Serpent's head (Gen 3:15).

When Goliath stood in that valley, defying God and harassing God's people, he was clothed in armor, but not just any armor. He was clothed in armor made of "scales (v. 5)." He looked like a huge serpent. When the rock flew from David's sling, it headed right toward the giant serpent's head, and he fell face down in the dust. Then David grabbed the giant's sword and chopped off his head (v. 51). The champion had cut off the head of the serpent. What happened in that valley was a reminder of what God promised to do to Satan; it was a vivid picture of how the Messiah would crush the evil one.

In the story of David and Goliath, we are not David. Jesus is. Jesus is the champion, the one who goes between, fighting the battle too big for us to win. He stands in our place, and slays the great Serpent. This is not an underdog story—it is the story of a Ser-

Some battles cannot be won by human strength.

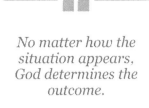

> No matter how the situation appears, God determines the outcome.

pent-crushing Savior who fights on our behalf. This story pulls us into the wonder of the Gospel. Jesus offers salvation to those who understand there is a battle with sin that they cannot win and judgment coming that they cannot escape. He takes our place, fighting for us, so that we can share in his victory.

Food for Thought When Goliath cursed David "by his gods" (v. 43), it did not make David fearful, but gave him confidence. David's God already had a showdown with the Philistine gods. It took place in chapter 5 when the ark of the covenant was captured by the Philistines. They placed the ark in the temple of their god, Dagon, and the next morning the idol of Dagon was bowing face down in front of the ark. This was a rematch, and Dagon did not stand a chance.

Faith in Action

Immediately after David's victory, the men of Israel stopped hiding behind rocks and rushed into the valley to fight the enemy. The winning side does not retreat. They move forward, chasing the darkness before them. Is there a person you have been afraid to tell about Jesus? Because of his victory, you do not need to fear. Commit to engaging them with the good news of sin's defeat and salvation's champion.

Prayer

Fearless Christian living is a testimony to the truth of the Gospel. When we stare into the face of death with unblinking eyes, our confidence validates the story of a risen and reigning King. Pray that God would give you courage to face the difficulties ahead.

Do You Want to Be King?

1 Samuel 18

One time while coaching my son's basketball team, I had a conversation with one of the referees. After very politely asking him about another missed call, he asked me a question: "Would you like to coach or would you like to ref?" I hesitated before answering to determine whether the question was rhetorical or if it was a genuine offer. Because if he was seriously asking, then I would have chosen to ref. My team would have played fine with someone else coaching, and I was quite certain the officiating would improve dramatically with someone else holding the whistle.

We have all probably been asked a similar question at some point. Maybe it was a parent asking us, "Do you want to be in charge?" Or a teacher asking, "Do you want to teach the class?" There is this part of us which bristles under someone else's authority, and so we challenge them. We think we could do a better job than they are doing. And perhaps we could do a better job than they do, but rebelling against authority leads to misery instead of joy. If I had answered that referee with, "Yes, I'd love to ref. I'm

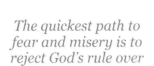

The quickest path to fear and misery is to reject God's rule over you.

quite certain I would do a better job than you're doing," it would not have led to our team flourishing.

In our study of 1 Samuel we have seen how the rule of King Saul was on the decline, while David, the one who would replace him as king, was on the ascent. God was with David and brought him success, yet Saul refused to humble himself and submit to God's authority. As David, God's chosen king, won victory after victory, Saul opposed him more and more.

This passage warns us about the danger of rejecting God's king. The quickest path to fear and misery is to reject God's rule over you. Like Saul, we are all tempted to cling to our independence, refusing to relinquish our autonomy, but that path only leads to misery. Do you want to be king over your life, king over your future, king over your destiny? If so, you can identify with Saul's struggle. But whenever you are tempted to reject God's rule over you, remember Saul's example and the grief that comes from a refusal to submit to God.

Chapter 18 is built around three truths. First, God exalts his chosen king, bringing him great success and fame. Second, the fool opposes God's king. Third, the wise adores God's king. Wisdom recognizes the matchlessness of the king God has chosen and joyfully offers him everything. There are two ways to relate to the king—God's chosen and anointed Messiah. You can oppose him or adore him. One way leads to misery and the other to victory.

God chose David, a shepherd boy from Bethlehem, to be the next king of Israel. After being anointed by Samuel (ch. 16), David won a great victory over the Philistine giant Goliath (ch. 17). That was just the start. Throughout chapter 18, we see his victories and fame continued to increase. God's favor on David was evident. Three times in this passage, we see that God was with David (vv. 12, 14, 28). Because God was with David, David was successful. Four times David's success is mentioned in this chapter (vv. 5, 14, 15, 30). David was not a rising star; he was a supernova. Like King Midas, everything he touched turned to gold. His success was not in just one area of life, but "in everything (v. 5)," "in all his activities (v. 14)," and more than every other officer in Saul's service (v. 30). None of this success is attributed to natural ability or innate charisma on David's part. It is attributed to the anointing of God and the presence of God's Spirit. In other words, God was exalting David. This was God's work, and those closest to David could see it. As a result of God's presence and repeated success, the fame of David increased and his name became well-known (v. 30). God was preparing David to lead his people, and he was preparing his people to follow David's leadership.

If God was with David, bringing him success and exalting him, then it was utter foolishness to resist what God was doing. Saul saw what God was doing and set himself in opposition. Four times in chapter 18 he attempted to kill David. The first two were by throwing a spear at David (vv. 10—11). Failing to kill David directly with his own hand, Saul plotted to kill him indirectly (v. 17). Saul had promised his daughter's hand in marriage to anyone who killed Goliath, but he reneged on the promise and added a condition. David could have his daughter's hand in marriage if he won more battles, battles that could cost him his life. David humbly declined Saul's of-

There are two ways to relate to the king— God's chosen and anointed Messiah. You can oppose him or adore him.

> *Sin twists our perspective on what is good and desirable.*

fer, and Saul gave his daughter to another man in marriage. Later, Saul noticed another daughter, Michal, loved David, and so he attempted the same scheme a second time. This time he got some of his servants involved in the plot (vv. 20—22).

David again refused, but we learn why this time. He was poor and could not afford to marry a princess. In that time, the groom would negotiate a certain bride price with the father of the bride. The bride price for a king's daughter would be far too high for a lowly shepherd to pay. Saul saw this as a way to manipulate David even further. He set the price as one hundred dead Philistines (A quick note: this is described in violent, bloody language. We must keep in mind that the Philistines were enemies of Israel, constantly invading and fighting Israel under the banner of their pagan gods. The proof Saul asked for has both political and religious significance). Saul's goal had nothing to do with maintaining Israel's safety but was entirely about David. He hoped David would die trying to kill these Philistine soldiers. David did not die, but instead killed two hundred Philistines, brought the evidence to Saul, and married Saul's daughter. Saul's plan backfired. David was supposed to die, not become part of the royal family.

Look at how Saul's opposition to what God was doing had twisted his mind. By the end of the chapter he was actively hoping for a Philistine victory. He was hoping his bitter rivals would defeat an attachment of his finest soldiers. Sin twists our perspective on what is good and desirable. If insanity is detachment from reality, then sin is ultimate insanity. It warps what we value.

Saul foolishly opposed God's king, but not everyone followed his example. The wise adored David. Six times in this chapter we read that David was loved (vv. 1, 3, 16, 20, 22, 28). The way you respond to the king who slays the giant and brings blessing to all of God's people is to adore him. The greatest example of this is found in Saul's son, Jonathan (vv. 1—4). If anyone had a reason to view David with suspicion it was Jonathan. In chapters 13–14, Jonathan defeated the Philistines and was celebrated by Israel. But then David came on the scene and supplanted Jonathan. He achieved a greater victory and was honored with a greater celebration. Was Jonathan jealous? No. Neither was he worried about David replacing him, the heir to Saul's throne, as king. In fact, Jonathan took off all his princely robes and offered them to David. Jonathan was saying to David, "You will be the next king, and I submit to you." Whereas the kingly robe was torn from Saul (ch. 15), Jonathan gave it up because he saw one who was more worthy to sit upon the throne.

The people of Israel were delighted to have David as their king, because David won great victories and brought them peace (vv. 5, 16). Jesus has done the same for us. He won great victories, conquering sin, death, and hell through the cross and resurrection, and he brings us peace with God. When they saw David, they sang, danced, and shouted his praises, just as we do when we worship Jesus each week. When we understand what Jesus has done, adoring him is only natural.

Oppose Jesus or adore him? Which do you do? Opposing him makes as much sense as standing on the beach in the face of a tidal wave. You and your feeble oppo-

When we understand what Jesus has done, adoring him is only natural.

sition will be swept away. The quickest path to fear and misery is to oppose God's rule in your life. But adoring Jesus is like standing on that same beach on a calm day, overwhelmed by his immense power and awestruck by his beauty as wave after wave of blessing breaks at your feet. Do you really think you make a better king than Jesus?

Food for Thought David was not a threat to Saul. Instead he repeatedly brought blessing to both Saul and the nation Saul led. He killed giants and defeated armies that threatened Saul's realm. He personally played soothing music to help Saul when he did not feel well. David served Saul faithfully and made Saul's kingdom safer and more prosperous. So why did Saul want to kill David? The root cause of Saul's hatred of David was pride and resentment (vv. 6—9).

Faith in Action The desire to rule over our own lives is at the root of pride and jealousy. If you are single, are you ever jealous when a friend gets engaged? If you have not been able to have children, is it hard to rejoice when a friend announces the big news? If you struggle to make ends meet, do you look with longing at someone else's vacation? The root of these feelings is pride. At the deepest level it is a longing to be king. Examine the last time you were jealous. How did your jealousy reveal a desire to be king over your life?

Prayer To love the king as much as you love yourself means giving him everything that belongs to you (v. 4). It means giving him your hopes and dreams, your priorities and plans, your kids and their future, your spouse or your desire for a spouse. It means laying the next twenty or forty or eighty years at his feet and saying, "All of it belongs to you! I surrender all. I will hold nothing back." As you pray today, intentionally commit everything you have to the Lord, holding nothing back.

God Is Working

1 Samuel 19–20

It is difficult to think about realities that cannot be touched or seen. It is much easier to focus our vision on the familiar in front of us, all the while ignoring the unfamiliar. The stream of immediate sense experiences is constantly catching us in its swift current. But there is always more going on than our eyes see. We are powerfully reminded of the unseen hand of God at work as we observe these events in the life of David. As readers, we are allowed to peer beyond the seen to the unseen. These stories are crafted to show us what is really happening in the world. Saul's conflict with David was not an ancient soap opera. Though there are deceitful words, treacherous acts, and daring escapes, there was also a powerful and faithful God who was always working to fulfill his promises and bring his plan to pass. When the king picked up a spear and hurled it at David's head, God was at work. When David had to crawl out the window of his own home to escape the hit squad, God was at work. When Saul sent troops to arrest David, God was at work. When Jonathan shot arrows as a warning to David, God was at work. God is always working to bring his plan to pass.

Saul embarked on a quest to kill David (v. 1). His action set the stage for the rest of 1 Samuel. The book now follows David as he ran from the armies of Saul. How could God allow this to happen? It was God who chose David to be the next king (ch. 16). It was God who gave David a great victory over the giant Goliath (ch. 17), and it was God who gave the Philistine armies into the hand of David (ch. 18). If we wrote the story, David would ascend the throne at this very moment and enjoy a lengthy, prosperous, and peaceful reign. But that was not what God designed for him. God had a different path prepared for David

God would work on David's behalf, and he would work through unlikely people. Saul's hatred of David had ratcheted up, and he announced his intentions to those closest to him. He would no longer resort to sabotage or subtle manipulation to stop David. But his son did not share his opinion of David. Jonathan delighted in David. In spite of their vastly different backgrounds, an abiding brotherhood had formed between them. Having heard his father, Jonathan made a promise to David to defend him before his father (vv. 2—3). The last person in the world you would have expected to defend David was Jonathan. From an earthly perspective, he had the most to lose. Yet, God used this unlikely person to deliver David from Saul.

Jonathan appealed to Saul on David's behalf (vv. 4—7). His appeal was simple and straightforward. "Father, David is innocent, and to kill him would be sin. Plus, he has brought peace and prosperity to your kingdom. You would only harm yourself if you kill him." Saul listened to the wise counsel of his son, swore not to harm David, and welcomed David back into his presence. It appeared to be a happy ending, but things changed quickly. Again, David won a great victory for the people of God, and again Saul responded by trying to harpoon him (vv. 8—10). His oath to protect David did not last long. God gave David the victory, and he also gave Saul the evil spirit. He was working his plan both in giving David the victory and in causing him to flee.

The next person God used to rescue David was the king's daughter (vv. 11—17). God used the king's son and the king's daughter to rescue the king's greatest threat. In spite of her help in this situation, Michal is not presented in a great light. Not only did she accuse David of threatening to kill her, but her ruse also involved the use of an idol. Remember, it was Saul's intention to use Michal as a weapon to bring David down, most likely because she worshiped false gods. God used a faithful, upright man and a lying, idolatrous woman to deliver David. God is able to do whatever pleases him. He is never powerless in a situation. His hands are never tied. Interestingly, God often uses the most unlikely people to bring his plans to pass.

Not only does God work through unlikely people, but also God works in unexpected ways. If using the king's son and daughter to deliver David was unexpected, then what happens next was even more unlikely. God caused each of Saul's hit squads to start prophesying, and when Saul showed up, the Spirit of God came upon him and he started prophesying too (vv. 18—24). It was a bizarre and unexpected means of deliverance.

God often uses the most unlikely people to bring his plans to pass.

Chapter 20 continues the theme of David escaping from Saul. Instead of four escapes like

> *God works in unexpected ways.*

chapter 19, there is only one. David and Jonathan developed a system for Jonathan to warn David about Saul's attempts on his life (20:1—23). Jonathan and Saul had a confrontation over David's absence from a meal, and Saul realized Jonathan was protecting David. Just as he did with David, Saul attempted to kill Jonathan (vv. 24—34). After what happened, Jonathan warned David, pledged his loyalty to him again, and encouraged him to run from Saul (vv. 35—42). God was continuing to work to bring his plan to pass. We get a better understanding of both the plan and a correct response by examining Jonathan's actions toward David.

The words of Jonathan (vv. 15, 42) remind us that God's plan is bigger than we can imagine. It is an eternal plan, written before the foundation of the world. It is an all-encompassing plan; every atom in the universe is included. It is a grand plan, which began with the creation of a new world and will end in a restored world. God's plan was to establish David's kingdom, an eternal kingdom, where he would bless those who blessed him and curse those who cursed him. God's plan for the world has always been to raise up a son of David who would bring blessing to the people of God and utterly destroy the enemies of God. The dividing line of humanity is how a person stands in relation to this Son.

Jonathan not only reminds us about God's plan, but he also provides us an example of how we should respond. Jonathan aligned himself with David (vv. 13—14, 42), and in doing so brought himself into submission to the plan of God. Like Jonathan, you need to align yourself to the Son of David, the Greater David, Jesus Christ, and in doing so submit yourself to God's great plan. Embracing Jesus Christ means turning from your sin, denying yourself the throne, and may even mean severing human relationships (Lk 14:26). Like Jonathan, you must choose to submit to God's plan even if it means your father is angry and attempts

Following Christ means he alone has your allegiance. He is the object of your supreme devotion.

to kill you. Following Christ means he alone has your allegiance. He is the object of your supreme devotion.

Food for Thought Years later, David wrote a psalm about these difficult times. He wrote: "O my Strength, I will sing praises to you, for you, O God, are my fortress, the God who shows me steadfast love (Ps 59:17)." It is often in difficult times—times of distress and darkness—that we come to understand God's strength and his care. When everyone forsakes us, in those moments, we understand God's faithful love in new and profound ways.

Faith in Action

Whatever you face this week, be encouraged that God is always working to bring his plan to pass. Though you may not know the specific steps he has planned for you, you can be certain that he is God, he is good, and he is leading you to greater faith in Jesus Christ. Do not let your circumstances overwhelm your vision. Look past them to our faithful God who is working all things together for your good and his glory.

Prayer

When times are difficult, we are tempted to pray for God to show us why we are suffering. We want to know the reason behind it. If you are facing difficulty, instead of asking "Why?" ask "How?" Ask God, "How can I bring glory to you through this difficulty?" Pray that God will give you clarity to see how to praise him in the midst of your trying circumstances.

Trusting God in Tough Times

1 Samuel 21:1–22:5

I love ice tea, but once in a while I go to the fridge to get a glass and realize the pitcher is empty. There is a sinking feeling in my stomach when I see the empty pitcher. I am going to have to wait to get a glass of tea. The reason I have to wait is because there is only one way to get a good glass of ice tea. To get a glass of ice tea, you have to put a teabag in hot water and wait. Time and heat cause the flavor inside the bag to come out. Most tea bags look the same, but as any tea lover will tell you, there are more varieties of tea than you can imagine. When you put that ordinary looking tea bag in hot water, you may get a standard glass of black tea or a fancy tea with lemon and jasmine. The difference is not the water—it's what's inside the bag. The hot water only draws the flavor out.

Each of us is like a tea bag. When we find ourselves in hot water, what is inside comes out. Time and heat reveal what is going on inside our hearts. Just as the hot water does not create the tea but merely reveals the tea, so too trials and difficulties in life do not create our re-

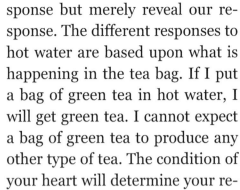

The condition of your heart will determine your response to the difficulties of life.

sponse but merely reveal our response. The different responses to hot water are based upon what is happening in the tea bag. If I put a bag of green tea in hot water, I will get green tea. I cannot expect a bag of green tea to produce any other type of tea. The condition of your heart will determine your response to the difficulties of life. Having studied both Saul and David, we are already aware of their heart condition. David was a man after God's own heart, and Saul was not. Saul was man after Saul's own heart.

In these two chapters, both men were faced with difficulties; both found themselves in varying levels of hot water. How did they respond? Our examination of David teaches us how we should respond, and our examination of Saul provides us warnings about how we might respond and what that response reveals about the condition of the heart.

David was faced with a number of difficulties. The first was no food (vv. 1—6). This episode began a 10-year exile for David. He would be on the run from Saul for nearly a decade. When you are in the middle of a lengthy trial, remember David's experience here and God's faithfulness to him. David headed to Nob, the city of priests, and asked the high priests for help. David was in such desperate need for food that he had to get the holy bread, the bread of Presence, to feed himself and the men he was meeting. David's heart was revealed in his commitment to holiness (v. 5). Roving bands of soldiers were not generally known for their chastity. That seems to be what the priest was suggesting with his question about their suitability to eat the bread. David's response was remarkable: "whenever the men are with me, we all keep ourselves holy." This was truly a man after God's heart; he was a man who longed to please God above all else. The second difficulty for David was that he had no weapons (vv. 8—9). In David's haste to flee from Saul, he did not even get the opportunity to grab weapons to defend himself. Thankfully, the priest had the sword of Goliath. Not a bad backup weapon.

David had no food, no weapon, and no home (v. 10). With no place else to go, David had to flee to Gath, which happened to have been Goliath's hometown. Who in their right mind would try to hide in the hometown of their most hated enemy? Saul's hatred of David was so strong that he had to flee the country. David assumed that the last place anyone would look for him would be in Gath. It was a savvy decision, except that the people of Gath recognized him and hauled him before the king (vv. 11—12). David had to pretend to be insane in order to escape (vv. 13—15).

In running from one hunter, David had fallen into the hands of another. Do not gloss over David's troubles. We easily turn the real people in biblical accounts into two dimensional characters. Because we know how the story ends, we act as if their struggles were not real. David's difficulties were just as real as yours. When he wrote, "You have kept count of my tossings; put my tears in your bottle (Ps 56:8)," he was referring to real tears and real sleepless nights. How would you sleep if you were on the run for your life, without food, weapons, or home, and all because you did what was right?

David's final difficulty may have been the most discouraging. He had no army (22:1—5). He had only four hundred men, and these four hundred men were either dis-

> *David's difficulties were just as real as yours.*

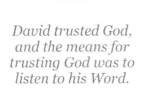

David trusted God, and the means for trusting God was to listen to his Word.

tressed, bankrupt, or disgruntled. It seems as if these men might have been more of a headache then an asset. At this point, David's situation seemed hopeless. It was so bad that he was even forced to relocate his family to Moab to keep them safe (vv. 3-4). It seems odd that David would send them to Moab for safe-keeping. Moab was not known for its friendliness to Israel. But who was David's great-grandmother? It was a woman from Moab named Ruth—a faithful woman who turned from worshiping idols to worship the true God. Once again, we see the amazing way God works. Generations earlier, his act of saving Ruth prepared the way for David's family to be kept safe during his exile.

Having seen David's difficulties, notice his response. How does a man after God's own heart respond to hot water? What was his reaction to the heat? David's response was to trust God and listen to his Word (v. 5). His foremost concern was what God wanted. He quickly and humbly submitted himself to the word of the prophet. He did not rationalize or revise God's commands. In times of difficulty, he turned to God. David trusted God, and the means for trusting God was to listen to his Word. His trust for God was displayed through his obedience to God's Word.

Where do you run in times of difficulty? Where do you flee in moments of fear and anxiety? Where you go for help reveals your god. Do you flee to someone? Do you look for an internal source of strength? If we trust God in the

Where you go for help reveals your god.

difficult times, our hope will spring from his Word. Like David did, we will find the presence, power, and peace of God through his Word.

Food for Thought The reality that a heart after God's is a heart that trusts him and listens to his Word has been repeated over and over throughout 1 Samuel. The difference between Samuel and Eli had to do with their reception of God's Word, and now we see this same striking difference between David and Saul. David's foremost concern was what God wanted. He quickly and humbly submitted himself to the word of the prophet.

Faith in Action

David said, "When I am afraid, I put my trust in you. In God, whose word I praise, in God I trust; I shall not be afraid. What can flesh do to me (Ps 56:3–4) ?" Who do you trust when you're afraid? Fill in the blank: When I am afraid, I put my trust in _____. It is easy to trust our effort, our spouse, our job, or our abilities instead of God.

Prayer

Read Psalm 56 and meditate on David's faith-filled response to difficulty. Re-write the psalm in your own words as a prayer you could pray in times of difficulty. Personalize the fight you are in (v. 1) and the adversaries you face (v. 2). Be honest about your struggles, then take your struggles to God in prayer.

Excusing Our Sin

1 Samuel 22:6–23

In the previous chapter, we saw how David's difficulties motivated a response of faith and obedience. Now we see the contrast with Saul. Before we see Saul's response, let's first examine Saul's difficulties. Saul's first difficulty was David (vv. 6–7). Again, we discover Saul sitting with spear in hand (v. 6). The irony should not be lost on us. The reason David was a problem for Saul was because of Saul's own actions. David had not attempted to kill Saul. All he had done was win great victories for Saul. Saul was the aggressor. Saul was the hunter.

Saul's second difficulty was related to the first. It was loyalty (v. 8). Saul imagined a vast conspiracy to take his throne. In his mind, David had masterminded a plan to ambush him, and his son Jonathan was in on the plan. All of his closest military leaders had been promised fields and vineyards if they aligned themselves with David. Of course, none of this was true.

Saul's example reminds us that some of the difficulties we face in life are simply the consequences of our sin. Not every difficulty is the result of our sin, but some dif-

> *Some of the difficulties we face in life are simply the consequences of our sin.*

ficulties are. When you are faced with a difficult situation your first move should be to suspect yourself. Am I reaping the consequences of a sinful action? Is this the direct consequence of my sin? If Saul had responded by suspecting himself, his difficulties could have been quickly and easily resolved. Confession and reconciliation would have remedied the difficult situation. Dark valleys are an invitation to self-examination. View each difficult situation as a hand-engraved invitation from your Creator to examine your heart. We know the condition of Saul's heart. We know his heart pursued his own agenda, not God's. So, it comes as no surprise that his response to difficulties was different than David's. What is in the teabag always comes out in hot water. David trusted God and listened to his Word. But Saul trusted himself and listened to his own word.

In Saul's view, Saul was in charge of Saul. What the prophet said no longer mattered, because the final authority in Saul's life was himself. From his perspective, he alone was looking out for his welfare, so he alone could be trusted. If a person does not turn to God for help, then where else is there to turn? The only other option is to turn inward—to trust our own ability, wisdom, or instincts. Even if we turn to another person for help, it is because we have determined they are better able to help us than God. Either way, we have assumed ultimate authority in our lives.

Saul's actions reveal a very common progression when we listen to ourselves. As we see it in these verses, consider whether or not it is familiar to you. First, Saul viewed himself as the victim (vv. 7–8). He basically said, "It could not be my fault. Everyone is against me. No one cares about me." Whenever we listen to ourselves, this is where we begin. We are quick to assume authority, but slow to accept responsibility. We think it is always the other person's fault. In difficult situations, if you find yourself blaming others, beware. You have begun to listen to yourself instead of God. You are not a victim. You are a sinner. You have a heart that is sinful and rebellious. God's voice will never lie to you and say, "You are not to blame. You could never do that." God will tell you the truth. God will never point you to your own righteousness. So if you find yourself admiring your good works or touting your moral superiority, you are not listening to God.

The second step in his downward progression is that Saul trusted foolish counselors (vv. 9–10). He listened to Doeg, a man from Edom. The Edomites were enemies of Israel. Throughout the Old Testament, they stand, almost proto-typically, as those opposed to God and his people. The King of Israel should not have been listening to the advice of an Edomite. Why did he? Because Doeg told him what he wanted to hear. When you listen to yourself, you first turn yourself into an innocent victim, then you find those who will say what you want them to say. At this point, you do not care about the truth. You only care about agreement. You will listen to anyone, as long as they agree with you.

Third, Saul made wild accusations (vv. 11–15). He accused the priests of conspiring with David (v. 13). If you are always the victim, and you are listening to fools who always agree with you, then what is to stop you from making wild accusations? In this case the answer was nothing. Even though the explanation from

Dark valleys are an invitation to self-examination.

> *We are quick to assume authority, but slow to accept responsibility.*

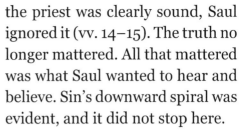

the priest was clearly sound, Saul ignored it (vv. 14–15). The truth no longer mattered. All that mattered was what Saul wanted to hear and believe. Sin's downward spiral was evident, and it did not stop here.

Fourth, Saul acted with sinful abandon (vv. 16–19). Saul commanded his servants to kill the priests, but they refused (vv. 16–17). So he turned to Doeg, who happily obeyed and slaughtered eighty-five priests (vv. 18–19). In the greatest irony of all, what Saul refused to do to God's enemies the Amalekites—thoroughly wipe them out—he did to the priests of God (ch. 15). This is the progression of sin; It begins with excuses and ends with destruction.

This progression was not unique to Saul. The husband who leaves his family begins by seeing himself as the victim. His marriage is struggling, and he does not listen to God's Word. He listens to himself. He believes his wife is to blame for all of the problems in their marriage. Instead of seeking help from godly counselors, he finds people who will agree with him. They encourage his warped perspective. They say exactly what he wants to hear. No matter what his wife does, he sees it as an attack on him. He makes wild accusations about her actions. He assumes the worst. Finally, he has justified his decision to move out and to move in with another woman. This is the path sin takes, and it is deadly.

In spite of Saul's sin, this passage ends with a glimmer of hope. David, the man after God's own heart, extended protection to the weak (vv. 20—23). In this, he demonstrated the heart of God. God, majestic and holy, transcendent and powerful, cares deeply for the weak. In David's weakness, he discovered God was his refuge, and here he extended that same care to another in his time of weakness. No matter our weakness, we can run to God for help. As you consider your heart, as you think about how you have responded to difficulties, maybe the hot water has exposed some dark and ugly

This is the progression of sin; It begins with excuses and ends with destruction.

things. No matter what sin has been revealed, you can run to God. In times of distress and difficulty, trust God and listen to his Word. You may find yourself frustrated and discouraged with what the hot water has revealed, but God is your refuge. Run to him.

Food for Thought

Psalm 1 teaches us that blessing comes when we receive counsel from the law of the Lord instead of the mouth of fools. David and Saul provide a living example of what the psalm teaches. Consider the lifestyle of those who you turn to for counsel in dark times. Do you look for someone to be honest with you or someone who agrees with you? Wisdom and blessing comes from listening to wise, biblical counsel.

Faith in Action

The church should be a place where we are committed to telling each other the truth, even if it is not what we want to hear in the moment. God gives you brothers and sisters in the church to sharpen and protect you, not to quietly go along with you when you are thinking foolishly. Have you joined a church? Are you building relationships? Are you listening to those who will help you think biblically?

Prayer

Pray for those in your church that you know are in seasons of difficulty. Pray for them to trust God and listen to his Word. Pray that God will protect them from temptation and foolish counsel. Send them a note to let them know you prayed for them today.

Mind the Gap
Part 1

1 Samuel 23

I stopped in London on my way to teach overseas. While there, I rode the underground train. Plastered everywhere was the warning: "Mind the Gap." It was painted on the floor, hung on the walls, and announced over the loudspeaker. If a station is built along a curved part of the track, a gap is created between the platform and the train. "Mind the Gap" was developed as a simple, memorable way to warn passengers to pay attention to their step on and off the train. The reason the phrase is written in many places in varying font sizes and colors is because passengers can easily forget that very significant gap, and forgetting the gap can be dangerous.

There exists a gap in life that we often forget about--a gap that deserves our attention; a gap, that if forgotten, results in great danger; a gap that mankind has always struggled with; a gap we fail to mind. It is the gap between deity and humanity. God is God, and we are not. But, we often want to be. Sin was born when the Serpent tempted Eve to erase the gap between man and God. Idolatry

> *God is God, and we are not.*

exists because we want to create gods more like us—obscuring the infinite gap between deity and humanity.

As we continue to study the story of Saul and David, we are confronted with the gap between man and God. This passage teaches us to mind the gap by unveiling the finite limits of humanity against the backdrop of God's infinite ability. The universal authority of God stands in stark contrast to the feeble authority of man. In 1 Samuel 23–24, the author uses an interesting storytelling device to highlight the gap between deity and humanity. Eighteen times he mentions someone's hand—either a man's or God's. A man's hand is a picture of his power. The contrast is between man's power, seen in either ability or authority, and God's power. In a face-off between the hand of man and the hand of God, the hand of God will always prevail, because there is an infinite gap between God's hand and man's.

At the end of chapter 22, David had attracted a small company of distressed, disgruntled men. Together, they were fleeing from the murderous pursuit of Saul. David heard about a band of Philistines attacking Israel (v. 1), and so he sought God's will before making a decision about whether to go and fight (v. 2). He was a man after God's own heart, and that trait was displayed in his refusal to enter battle without first seeking the will of God. Though David was running for his life, he was still being used by God to rescue the people of God. He is portrayed in this passage as the savior of Israel. He was God's chosen means of deliverance. Through David, God brought deliverance and safety to His people.

David's army was terrified about fighting the Philistines (v. 3). They were undermanned (there were only 600 of them) and were already fleeing for their safety. They had no desire to be caught between two armies hoping to extinguish them. Again, David sought the Lord's will. The response returned the same. He was to go and save the city, and he did. He won a great victory and delivered the citizens of Keilah from the armies of the Philistines (vv. 4—5). David realized the only reason his hand was able to conquer the Philistines was because of God's promise to give him the victory. The hero in this rescue was not David—the hero was David's God. The hand of David was successful, but David knew it was God's doing.

After Saul massacred the priests in Nob, the one surviving priest, Abiathar, fled to David (v. 6). In his hand, he carried the ephod. The ephod was part of the priestly garments. In the pockets of the ephod were two stones, the Urim and Thummim. God often used these stones to reveal his will to the priests. Here we observe that David was the one who was actively seeking the will of God. Saul, on the other hand, was listening only to himself and those who went along with his foolish ideas, like Doeg the Edomite. It should have been Saul who rescued the people of Kielah from the Philistines. After all, he was the king. Not only did he fail to rescue them (because of his obsession with David), but also he viewed David's victory as an opportunity to kill him (vv. 7—8). Saul said: "God has given him into my hand (v. 7) " As is true of most error, there was a kernel of truth in this statement. Saul was correct that only God could do this, but he was completely mistaken about what was happening. God was not

Idolatry exists because we want to create gods more like us—obscuring the infinite gap between deity and humanity.

God's ability is not limited.

providing Saul the opportunity to kill David.

Again, David turned to God for help (vv. 9–11). He sought God's wisdom. His questions revealed his confidence in God's power. He asked God if the people he had just rescued would turn and hand him over to Saul's hand. David's understanding of the gap between God's hand and man's was clear. God knew and determined the future. Unlike man, God's ability is not limited. The ultimate reason Saul's hunt for David failed was because God did not give David into his hand (v. 14).

When David was in a situation that could have been discouraging, Jonathan came and encouraged him by strengthening his hand in God (vv. 16–18). In this continuing metaphor of the hand, we see David's hand was dependent on God. His strength came not from himself, but from another. How did Jonathan go about strengthening the hand of David in God? He began by reminding David there was no reason to fear. Saul was powerless to hinder the plan of God. He said, "My father Saul will never lay a hand on you (v. 17). " Because God had anointed David as king, Saul was powerless to stop him.

We cannot strengthen someone's hand in God by assuring them of their own ability to handle difficult circumstances; that is a fool's hope. You will face problems that are greater than you are. For the moment, Saul's hand was greater than David's, and so was Goliath's before him. But no one's hand was greater than God's. Confidence in trials should never come from within. You are not strong enough to handle everything that comes your way. You need help. You need God's hand at work. Many

Psalms speak of God as our refuge, fortress, shield, strong tower, deliverer, strength, rock, and help, because our strength comes, not from within, but from without. We need an external source of power to overcome the difficulties of life. Our strength is limited. God's strength is limitless.

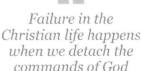

Failure in the Christian life happens when we detach the commands of God from the promises of God

The next verses (vv. 19–29) reveal that God's hand was at work delivering David from the hand of Saul. Saul continued to hunt for David, and just when he was about to catch him, a messenger informed him of a Philistine raid. He was forced to stop hunting David in order to deal with the Philistines. The Philistines attacked when they did because God would not give David into Saul's hand (v. 14). Once again, God protected David and thwarted the evil plans of Saul.

Food for Thought David, the promised king, was in the middle of a period of great suffering. He had no place to lay his head, and he was on the run for his life from the leaders of Israel, yet David rescued a host of people from death. In spite of his rescue, they still turned their back on him, willing to betray him to the enemy. Does that sound familiar? David's suffering while delivering his people reveals a glimpse of the coming king of Israel, who would suffer to save the people of God.

Faith in Action

Behind the command of God stands the promise of God. He commands David to "Go," and he promises to give the Philistines into David's hand. Failure in the Christian life happens when we detach the commands of God from the promises of God, like taking the battery out of your car and being dismayed when it will not run. The promises of God are the power source to obey the commands of God. Are you embracing the promises of God as the power source for obeying his commands?

Prayer

As you pray for strength to obey the commands of God, rehearse his promises to you. Begin by praying for help to make disciples, but do so based upon the promise that Jesus will be with you wherever you go (Mt 28:19—20). The promise empowers the command.

Mind the Gap
Part 2

1 Samuel 24

In the eighth grade, my teacher gave my class an assignment to write a short essay on what we wanted to do with our lives. We were to decide on a vocation, discuss why we chose it ,and take a picture of ourselves dressed up in the appropriate clothing. As a young Nostradamus, I accurately predicted my future as a professional basketball player. If it had not been for my lack of height, skill, and athletic ability, I would have made it to the NBA! Even at the time, I knew the possibility of playing professional basketball was slight, but it did not keep me from dreaming. Part of growing up was learning to recognize the sizable gap between my desire and my ability. There were a number of things I wanted to do, but could not. I had to learn to identify that gap between fantasy and reality.

The ongoing struggle between Saul and David reminds us of the gap between God and man. I am much closer to being a professional basketball player than I am to being God. The gap in both ability and authority between God and man is infinite. The previous chapter showed

> *Even though God has promised the kingdom to David, it was not up to David to take it.*

the difference in ability between man's hand and God's hand. This chapter reveals the gap in authority between God and man, as Saul overstepped his authority, while David humbly recognized the authority of God.

Saul stepped out in pursuit of David with 3,000 of his most capable soldiers. As they got near David's last known location, Saul entered a cave to use the bathroom. But the cave was not empty—David and his men were hiding deep inside it (vv. 1—3). I found this event encouraging when we were languishing in a potty-training battle with one of our sons. It was a good reminder that God is in control of everything; even intestines answer to God.

David's men encouraged him to either kill or capture Saul while he was using the bathroom. They took his presence in the cave as a sign that God had delivered Saul into David's hand. David refused to harm Saul, however, choosing instead to sneak up and cut loose a piece of Saul's robe (v. 4). He was immediately overcome with regret. He told his men that he should not have cut the robe and refused to let them capture Saul (vv. 5—7).

David's regret at cutting Saul's robe can be traced back to chapter 15. In chapter 15, the prophet Samuel informed Saul that his kingdom had been taken from him. Saul fell to the ground pleading with Samuel, and when he fell he tore the corner from Samuel's robe. Samuel turned to Saul and told him that just as the robe was torn, Saul's kingdom would be torn from him. When David cut off that piece of Saul's robe, the significance was clear. The kingdom was being taken by David. Yet, as David told his men, the kingdom was not his to take. God anointed Saul, and

God was the only one who had the authority to deal with Saul. David recognized the gap between God's authority and his own. Even though God has promised the kingdom to David, it was not up to David to take it.

Christians should not be known as those who take what they want. We should be known as those who wait patiently for God to give us what we need. As Paul reminded the Corinthians: "What do you have that you did not receive (1 Cor 4:7)?" Our attitude needs to be the attitude of Job: "Naked I came from my mother's womb, and naked shall I return. The LORD gave, and the LORD has taken away; blessed be the name of the LORD (Job 1:21)." Job got it. He understood God was the only one who had the authority to give and to take. God alone reserves that right. The believer who assumes the authority to take what he believes is rightfully his has attempted to usurp the throne and depose the true King.

David followed Saul out of the cave to plead his innocence (vv. 9–15). He had multiple opportunities to kill Saul and refused to take them. Why? Because judgment belonged to God, not David (v. 12). David refused the temptation to judge Saul. He left the matter in God's hand. He was certain God was both willing and able to tell the difference between right and wrong. God did not need David's help delivering a verdict.

Do you trust God to judge those who sin against you? Or do you feel that you have the right, maybe even the responsibility, to set things straight? There is a universal temptation to climb up on the judge's bench and right the wrongs that others are doing. God is doing just fine. He does not need you to try cases for him. He

> *The believer who assumes the authority to take what he believes is rightfully his has attempted to usurp the throne and depose the true King.*

The life of the believer should be characterized by asking for help.

saw what that person did to you, and he heard what they said about you. He was not asleep when they hurt you. You do not have to repay them. God is more than capable of judging sin.

When Saul heard what David said, he began to weep. He confessed his own sin and acknowledged that David would become the next king of Israel (vv. 16—20). Saul's momentary change in heart did not come about because of David's military might. God protected David. As David yielded to God's authority, God intervened on his behalf, again rescuing him from danger.

Minding the gap in ability between God and you frees you to ask for help. Because David trusted in God's hand and not his own, he was free to be weak. Three different times in these two chapters he asked for help. When you are on God's side, you do not have to be superman because someone greater than superman upholds you. If you struggle to ask for help, it means you are unwilling to admit your weakness. An unwillingness to ask for help is a sure sign you still maintain some confidence in your own ability. The life of the believer should be characterized by asking for help.

Minding the gap in authority between God and you frees you to show mercy. We are not responsible for judging those who sin. Because you trust God to judge, you are free to show mercy. You can love that co-worker who is cruel to you. You can forgive the family member who is inconsiderate. You can be merciful to

You are not the king, but you serve a king with unmatched ability and ultimate authority.

the selfish member of your small group. You can pour out mercy on others, because you know God rules forever in righteousness and justice. Be diligent to mind the gap. You are not the king, but you serve a king with unmatched ability and ultimate authority.

Food for Thought *We often want to judge the person who sins against us. But what is true for the person who sins against you is true for you too. You deserve to be judged for your sin. We all deserve judgment because we are lawbreakers, and we will all stand before this Judge one day—a day Scripture refers to as the Judgment Day. On that day, he will either sentence you or pardon you. Carefully consider how you stand before him for you will stand before him. On the day God judges you, what will the verdict be?*

The gospel is the good news that sinners can **Faith in Action** *be forgiven. It is especially good because the sin you see most is your own sin. You may choose to ignore it, but you are the worst sinner you know. Jesus died in your place, so that he could forgive your sin. If you are angry over someone sinning against you, remember you have sinned much more against Jesus. Is there someone you need to forgive just like Jesus forgave you? Contact them today and let them know that you have forgiven them because you have been forgiven by him.*

Prayer

When was the last time you asked God for help? We are needy, and God is wealthy. So we should turn to him for help. What do you need help with today? Maybe there is someone you need to forgive or someone you need to ask forgiveness from. God will help you. Ask him right now.

Correct Posture

1 Samuel 25

How important is correct posture? At times, the correct posture can be the difference between life and death. About 2,500 years ago, three men (Shadrach, Meschach, and Abednego) were commanded to kneel and worship before a large idol. Their decision not to adopt the required posture almost cost them their lives. They were thrown into a fire, and if God had not rescued them, they would have died (Dan 3). A similar fate has fallen on many since that time who refused to take the posture required by those in authority over them.

In this chapter we see another example that correct posture can save your life. The difference between life and death is your posture toward God and his anointed king. David, who had been anointed the future king of Israel, was on the run from Saul, the current king of Israel. David had an opportunity to kill Saul, but he refused to take it, and instead left vengeance in God's hands. Soon after sparing Saul's life, David had a run-in with a fool and decided to take vengeance into his own hands. That is until he was stopped by a beautiful woman. This chapter has it all—conflict, threats, violence, and romance.

> *One of the marks of a fool is stinginess with the financial resources God gives.*

The two characters who interacted with David—one a fool and one wise—are a husband and wife, Nabal and Abigail (vv. 2—3). These two teach us a very important lesson about our posture toward God, and ultimately toward God's anointed king. David, who had been anointed as the shepherd king of Israel, points us ahead to Jesus, the ultimate shepherd king. Our posture toward Jesus is a matter of life or death. This story shows us two drastically different postures toward the king, which led to drastically different results.

The story took place during the time of year when sheep were being sheared; an event followed by a feast of thanksgiving. David, who was responsible to feed his six hundred men, sent a message to Nabal, a man who owned three thousand sheep. Essentially the message was this: "Over the past few months, my men and I have acted as guards over your flock of sheep. Not only did we not take any sheep for food, but we prevented others from doing so. Since the sheep have been delivered to you safely and have been shorn of their wool, will you provide some of them for us to eat (vv. 4—8)? Nabal, whose very name means "fool (v. 25)," took a foolish posture toward David. He not only refused to share any food with David and his men, but he insulted him. Nabal, like King Saul, set himself in opposition to the anointed king, and it led to his own death.

Nabal was harsh to others and dishonest in his business (v. 3). He had the condescending look which often characterizes a fool. He believed he was superior to others and treated others with disrespect. Have you ever been around someone who is harsh? The root cause of their harshness is arrogance. They do not want to waste their time with those they feel are beneath them. When David sent the messengers, he instructed them to show Nabal great respect. In verse 6, David called Nabal his brother, and in verse 8, he referred to himself as Nabal's son. David was adopting a posture of humility. But Nabal responded with smugness (v. 10). His condescension was so well-known that one of his servants mentioned it to Nabal's wife (vv. 15—17).

The fool feels no responsibility to be generous to others, because he sees no one as an equal. Instead of living with open and generous hands, the fool lives with clenched fists. He will not share his hard-earned resources with others. We see this is Nabal's response to David's request (v. 11). Nabal's number one priority was Nabal, and he operated under the delusion that he was solely responsible for his success. Did Nabal have enough to give something to David and his men? Yes. He not only had three thousand sheep and one thousand goats, but his wife, at a moment's notice, was able to pull together two hundred loaves of bread, two hundred cakes, two vats of wine, five butchered sheep, and various other treats and take them to David. One of the marks of a fool is stinginess with the financial resources God gives.

Nabal's ultimate problem was not how he treated other people or how he spent his money; these were symptoms of a greater problem. The greater problem was his unwillingness to bow his head to the rightful king. Nabal saw himself as a king (v. 36). His allegiance was only to himself. His posture toward the true king, David, was one of defiance. He would not bow his head to anyone. He illustrates the ultimate mark of a fool who

Where the posture of a fool leads to death and destruction, the posture of the wise leads to life and blessing.

> God's chosen King,
> Jesus, is your rightful
> lord.

believes there is no God (Ps 14:1). Nabal sowed foolishness and reaped destruction (vv. 37—39). So it is for everyone who refuses to bow before the true king.

In contrast with Nabal's foolishness, we see the wisdom of his wife, Abigail. Where the posture of a fool leads to death and destruction, the posture of the wise leads to life and blessing. Abigail was described as beautiful (v. 3) and discerning (v. 33). Discernment is what makes a person truly beautiful (Pr 1:22). Abigail's beauty came from wisdom, and her wisdom was revealed in her posture toward David, God's anointed king. When Abigail heard how Nabal treated David, she put together the world's largest gift basket and rushed out to meet David, hoping to avert the destruction she knew was coming upon her family (vv. 18–35). In that culture, an act of dishonor could lead to a blood feud. Nabal's caustic response to David was certainly strong enough to bring a violent response. When Abigail met David, her posture toward him was the opposite of Nabal's. She came, not with a condescending look, clenched fists, and unbowed head, but with a bowed head and bended knee.

Abigail recognized David's authority. She referred to David as "my lord" eleven different times in their conversation (vv. 26, 27, 28, 29, 30, 31, 41). She placed herself under his authority. This was not simply the result of David's military strength. It was the awareness of David's unique position as God's chosen king (vv. 28–31). Do you, like Abigail, recognize true authority in your life? God's chosen King, Jesus, is your rightful lord.

The wise do more than bow their head to the king. They also bend their knee. Bending the knee is the posture of worship and adoration. We bow the knee to swear allegiance to the king and to await his orders. In this passage, Abigail knelt before David and referred to herself as his servant eight different times (vv. 24, 25, 27, 28, 31, 41). Do you view yourself as the servant of Jesus Christ? If you are a Christian, you are a servant. Serving is not a burden, but a privilege. Jesus has the authority to tell us what to do, and our response should be immediate obedience. Four times in this passage, Abigail responded quickly to David (vv. 18, 23, 34, 42). She did not argue or complain, whine or negotiate. She obeyed immediately.

As we obey the king, we act in ways that reveal the king's priorities. Here, Abigail made peace between David and Nabal, preventing David from sinning and harming his future reign. In her obedience to the king, she acted more and more like the king acts. The more we submit to King Jesus, the more our actions reflect his actions and our priorities his priorities.

Throughout the book of 1 Samuel, we have seen how David was a picture of the Messiah. He was the shepherd king who conquered enemies and brought peace. In these ways, he pictured what Jesus would do one day. But in this passage, we are also reminded that David was not the Messiah. He anticipated the final king, but he was not the final king. The flaws that would cause David's downfall—women and murder—are introduced in this episode. This account ends with David taking multiple wives (vv. 42–44), a sin that would lead him to taking another man's wife in the future. But the heart of this passage is David's desire to take vengeance into his own hands. In the past, he trusted God to fight his battles for him, but this

> *The more we submit to King Jesus, the more our actions reflect his actions and our priorities his priorities.*

time he wanted to fight back. In this moment, we see how David was not like Jesus. When Jesus was mocked, he did not respond with vengeance. When Jesus was dishonored, he bore it silently. When Jesus was mistreated, he did not get angry. Because of his love for us, Jesus, the last and final King, who will rule forever over a renewed heaven and earth, suffered in our place.

Food for Thought *Jesus told his disciples a story about a man like Nabal (Lk 12:13—21). The man had been blessed by God with another good harvest—a harvest so good his barns were not big enough to store all the grain. Did he see the excess as an opportunity to use his resources to bless others? No, he tore down his smaller barns in order to build bigger barns. Jesus called him a fool. How easily we fall into the same perspective. We dream about bigger houses, nicer cars, fuller bank accounts, and longer vacations. We store up treasure for ourselves, instead of seeing our resources as opportunities to bless other people.*

Faith in Action *Nabal treated David's messengers like hungry soldiers treat a captured cow—he slaughtered them (cf. 14:32; 15:19). He cannibalized them with his sharp tongue. Feelings of superiority are exposed by critical speech. This is especially true in how we treat those serving us. How you treat a waitress, bus driver, or day laborer says a lot about how you view yourself. Nabal, a fool, treated others with condescension. How do you treat those who serve you?*

Prayer

Ask God to expose any areas of foolishness in your own life. Do you give a condescending look to certain people? Are you stingy with your money? Do you want to be king? Confess your foolishness and commit yourself to quick, joyful, and humble obedience. Ask God to give you an opportunity to be generous with someone today.

Courageous Confidence

1 Samuel 26—27

Leah Sharibu missed her 15th birthday party. Instead of being home to celebrate with her family and friends, she was being held prisoner by Boko Haram. Leah and 109 other girls from her school were kidnapped. The other 109 girls were released and reunited with their families—only Leah remains captive. The reason she is still held captive is because she refused to convert to Islam. Where does that kind of courage originate? There is one source of courage available to Christians at all times. It is not dependent on how we feel at the moment, and it does not require any particular set of skills. Whenever we face a situation which demands a courageous decision, we can act courageously, not by turning inward, but by turning to God. Courage comes from confidence in God.

Throughout our study of 1 Samuel, we have seen David act courageously in situation after situation. If you were to draw a picture of courage, you might draw a picture of young David defeating a lion or running into a valley to face a giant. David's courage was evident in multiple

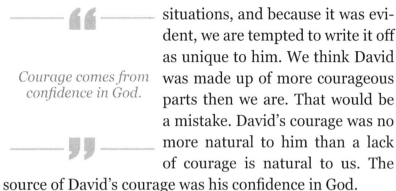

> *Courage comes from confidence in God.*

situations, and because it was evident, we are tempted to write it off as unique to him. We think David was made up of more courageous parts then we are. That would be a mistake. David's courage was no more natural to him than a lack of courage is natural to us. The source of David's courage was his confidence in God.

We find two examples of David's courage in chapter 26, and we also see the source of his courage. But then we see an example where David fails to act courageously. Chapter 26 is very similar to chapter 24. In both chapters King Saul was pursuing David, intent on killing him. And both times David was given an opportunity to kill Saul but refused to take it.

The first way David showed courage was in the face of an enemy. David was on the run with 600 men. These men were not Ivy-league educated entrepreneurs, but "desperate, in debt, or discontented (22:2)." Look who Saul brought with him to hunt David (v. 2). 3,000 triathletes. 3,000 of the fittest young men in Israel. This was not a fair fight. 600 broke, discontent desperadoes versus 3,000 Israeli, Ninja warriors. What should David have done? It was obvious. He should have found a cave and hid there until Saul gave up. What did David do? He sent out spies to see where Saul's army was (v. 4), and then he decided to go visit with two other men (v. 6) That was either a courageous decision or a foolish decision. The odds of three men versus three thousand were not in David's favor.

When David got to Saul's camp, he found everyone asleep. They were sleeping so deeply that the three of them strolled into camp and had a conversation right next to King Saul. Abishai wanted to kill Saul, but David forbid it (v. 12). After getting away from camp safely, David called down and conversed with Saul. Even though this was his second opportunity to kill Saul, he refused to harm him. In spite of what others had said, David had no interest in harming the king. He had always and only served the king and brought blessing to the kingdom. After hearing from David, Saul again confessed his foolishness and again promised never to hurt David. In an ironic twist, David returned Saul's spear to him, the spear that had so often been thrown at David in a futile attempt to end his life (v. 22).

Not only did David show courage in the face of an enemy, but he also showed courage in the presence of a friend (vv. 8—9). This was the second time David had to tell his friends not to harm Saul. In chapter 24, Saul walked into the cave that David and his men were hiding in and proceeded to use the restroom—he was in the most vulnerable position possible. David's men—his loyal companions—saw this as an opportunity from God for David to end the exile. But he refused to harm Saul or let any of his companions harm him. Standing up to your enemies is hard, but standing up to your friends is even harder. It took courage for David to walk into Saul's camp, but it took greater courage for David to restrain Abishai's hand.

The source of David's courage was his confidence in God. But it was not generic confidence in God, but specific truths about God that instilled confidence in David. David was confident that God was alive (vv. 10, 16). All around David were nations worshiping gods and goddesses carved out of stone. David contrasted their false gods with the true God—the living God. This

Standing up to your enemies is hard, but standing up to your friends is even harder.

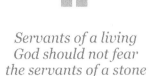

Servants of a living God should not fear the servants of a stone god.

is exactly what he said when he saw the giant, Goliath, taunting the armies of Israel (17:26). Servants of a living God should not fear the servants of a stone god.

David's courage came from his confidence that God was alive and that God would act on behalf of his people. God is not distant. He is not a heavenly chess player moving us about his board as pawns in his battle with evil. God acts in, through, and on behalf of his people. David was confident that God would act to right the injustice of Saul (vv. 10, 23—24). We can act with courage because we know that we do not act alone. God is in heaven, but he is active on earth. Do you believe that God is active in your life? Too often we live with a type of practical atheism where we forget, ignore, or disbelieve that God cares about us and what is happening at the moment. Courage comes from confidence in God—he is alive and he is active.

Even someone as courageous as David—who stood up to a fearsome giant and a homicidal king—can fail to be courageous. In chapter 27, we see David's failure. When he focused on God and trusted God's Word, he had confidence to make courageous decisions. But we see what happened when he started to doubt (27:1). David lost confidence in God's protection and began to fear Saul's power. In his previous encounter with Saul, David trusted that God would bring an end to Saul (26:10), but now he feared that Saul would end him.

His lack of confidence in God led him to make a poor decision. He headed back to the city of Gath and sought refuge from the Philistine king. He chose to do very thing he feared (being forced to dwell in a land of idolatry—26:19). Focusing on his circumstances instead of his living God caused him to lose hope. Instead of trusting God to save him, something David had done so often in the past, he tried to save himself by aligning with the pagan king.

He and his men acted as mercenaries, fighting against the enemies of the Philistines. And David deceived the Philistine king into thinking he was fighting against Israel. This was a low point in David's exile. These sixteen months probably forced David to do some explaining when he returned to Israel after Saul's death. Why was the future king of Israel acting as a servant to Israel's greatest enemy, fighting his battles for him? The answer seems simple. David struggled to believe God would protect him. Instead of trusting God, he trusted himself. His lack of confidence led to a period of cowardly decisions.

In spite of David's lack of faith, God still used him during those months. The people he fought against were enemies of the Philistines, but they were also enemies of Israel. David was a new Joshua, defeating the enemies of God, the ones Joshua failed to defeat, and he eventually ushered in a period of rest unlike Israel had ever known (v. 8).

In this way, David points us to Jesus—the perfect King who defeats the enemies of God and offers rest unlike anyone has ever known. Years later, David would sit down on the throne, having brought peace and rest to the kingdom, but Jesus offers each of us a greater peace and a greater rest (Mt 11:28). The ultimate source of courage comes through faith in Jesus; the one who defeated death and hell invites you to life in his kingdom. He invites you to lay down your arms and rest. We can be courageous

God acts in, through, and on behalf of his people.

because the battle has already been fought, the outcome decided, and the victory secured.

Food for Thought The gospel of Jesus Christ does not encourage you to defeat fear through confidence in your ability, your potency, or your destiny. When you are decisive, is it due to confidence in yourself or confidence in God? The end goal is not simply confident decisions, but courageous decisions motivated by confidence in God. Only confidence in God is an act of faith, and only confidence in God can sustain you when things do not go as planned.

After the crucifixion of Jesus, his disciples huddled in a second-story room with locked doors, fearful of what might happen to them. *Faith in Action* Two months later, they were sent home from a beating, and on the way home they sang and shouted with joy. What happened? Jesus was alive. They served a living God. When they were tempted to fear, they thought about Jesus' victory over death and found courage to face whatever was ahead. Why does the resurrection give us courage? Because if Jesus has conquered death, what weapon does anyone have that can truly intimidate us?

Prayer

In Psalm 18, David called the Lord his strength, rock, fortress, deliverer, refuge, shield, and salvation. David never mentioned his own ability, insight, or knowledge. His confidence in God produced courage in difficult circumstances. What difficult circumstances are you facing right now? Meditate on Psalm 18:1—3 and ask God for courage to obey him even in the tough moments.

The Downward Spiral of Sin

1 Samuel 28

I remember reading the story about a snake that went missing at New York's Bronx Zoo. This was not any snake. It was an Egyptian cobra. The venom of an Egyptian cobra is so deadly that it can kill a mature elephant in three hours and a human in fifteen minutes. What caught my attention in the story was how the zoo treated the snake's disappearance. It did not close the zoo. It did not evacuate all of the visitors. It merely posted a sign on the locked door of the reptile exhibit which read: "The World of Reptiles is closed today. Staff observed an adolescent Egyptian cobra missing from an off-exhibit enclosure on Friday." That hardly seems like enough warning to me. If an earthworm escaped that might be fine. But an Egyptian cobra? A sign on a locked door is not enough.

There is a principle that comes into play in a situation like this—a principle ignored by the zoo staff. The greater the danger, the louder the warning. The warning should match the danger. Today's study is a warning, not

> *The greater the danger, the louder the warning.*

uttered quietly, but shouted at full volume. Nothing is more dangerous than sin. Nothing deserves a greater warning than sin. We are nearing the end of 1 Samuel. King Saul is about to meet his tragic end. Chapter 28 provides a powerful warning about the deception and destruction of sin.

The Philistines were gathered for war against Israel (v. 1), and Saul was afraid (v. 5). Saul's reaction to the Philistine army was similar to his reaction to the appearance of Goliath in chapter 17. He was paralyzed by fear. We have to wonder if his fear would have been as great if David had been there to lead the army. Every time David had picked up a weapon to fight the Philistines, he had won a great victory. Of course, the reason David was not there was because Saul had driven him away.

Without David and in great fear, Saul turned to the Lord, but all he heard was silence (v. 6). Why did Saul want to inquire of God? Was it driven by a heart that wanted to please God? A longing to serve him? A commitment to obey? No. Saul wanted God like most of us want a rich uncle. Someone to write a check, free us from our debt, smile at our foolishness, and not hold us accountable. Why did Saul have such a difficult time communicating with God? David had a priest and prophet with him, but Saul had slaughtered the priests and severed his relationship with Samuel years earlier. The silence of God was the result of Saul's own actions.

Hearing only a hush from heaven, Saul told his servants to find a medium. Saul backtracked on his royal decree (v. 2) and sought out a witch—someone accomplished in the occult. We should not be surprised that Saul's advisors knew where one could be found. He had not exactly surrounded himself with wise, godly counsel. Saul had to convince the witch it was safe to perform her witchcraft (vv. 8—12). But when she did an old man appeared, and Saul recognized him as Samuel (v. 14).

How do we interpret Samuel's appearance? We are given few details, so we should not attempt to build a model of Old Testament eschatology from this passage. We should pay careful attention to the witch's shocked reaction. She was shocked, because she really did not expect to see anyone. To actually have a visit from a dead person was not what she expected. Her normal experience was probably a combination of deception and demonism.

Apparently Saul could see Samuel, but he could not hear him. Samuel, the prophet of God, did not need a witch to serve as his mouthpiece. Samuel offered Saul some information (vv. 15—19). Most of what he said was merely recapping what he had told Saul earlier. God had torn the kingdom from Saul and was giving it to David. This was happening because of Saul's disobedience to God when he refused to thoroughly defeating the Amalekites (ch. 15). The only new information was the date of Saul's death; it would happen the following day. Israel would lose in battle, and Saul and his sons would die.

The final act in the night's drama is delivered in a straightforward, matter of fact manner. You can feel the tension in the utter inevitability of Saul's death. It is like watching a prisoner on death row eat his last meal. There is a crushing sadness in Saul's final hours (vv. 20—25). There is very little commentary, just an aching sorrow in the report of Saul's actions. He knew what

Sin and faith never grow together because sin presents a false picture of God.

> *Sin always pushes us to view God from our perspective.*

was going to happen. He knew that Samuel's words would come true. The author did add one chilling reminder of why Saul was destined to this fate. Twice he used the word "obey." The witch obeyed Saul (v. 21), and then Saul obeyed her (v. 22). Saul, whose downfall was his failure to obey God, ended his time on earth by obeying the instructions of a witch.

The tragic failure of Saul should serve as a warning for us. As you consider his example and apply it to your own situation, notice five reasons you need to be warned about sin. First, sin distorts theology (v. 5–6). Sin is organically rooted to unbelief. Sin and faith never grow together because sin presents a false picture of God. When David saw Goliath, he responded with confidence in God. He viewed God correctly, and so his response was correct. But when Saul saw the Philistines lined up to fight Israel, he responded with great fear and trembling. He had no confidence in the power and protection of God. Sin always pushes us to view God from our perspective. Claiming to understand God from man's perspective is like claiming to understand the sun because you like to go to the beach. From your perspective on the beach, you can learn some things about the sun—it's hot and bright. But you have little idea how hot, or how bright, or how big it really is. Sin encourages us to view God as if he revolves around us, and not us around him.

Second, sin disregards truth (vv. 7–10). Saul had made a wise decision to banish the spiritists from Israel. However, sin caused him to disregard the truth of that earlier decision. Sin reverses biblical decisions. Whenever you need to wear a disguise and wait until nightfall, that is probably a bad sign. Whenever you have to hide what you are doing, it is because you have chosen to disregard the truth. Sin does not like the light. It does not like open, bright spaces. It likes cold, dark corners. It likes to be done in secret.

Sin downplays its real, painful, bitter consequences.

Third, sin downplays consequences (vv. 17–20). Saul was surprised by Samuel's statement, even though he had heard it before. Years earlier, Samuel had told him of the consequences of his sin. Saul was hoping that somehow he would escape sin's consequences. That is the false hope we hold to whenever we sin. We weigh the options and think, "I will not get caught. No one will know." We convince ourselves that we will get away with it. We are smarter than the people who get caught. Sin downplays its real, painful, bitter consequences.

Fourth, sin destroys life (v. 19). Saul and his sons would die because of his sin. Sin always brings death (James 1:14—15; Rom 6:23). There is an inescapable connection between sin and death. Sin is like a cobra's bite. No matter how big and strong you are, you are no match for sin's venom. It will bring you down.

Fifth, sin deceives slowly. Do you think Saul would have ever imagined himself consulting a witch for help? No way. Not in a million years. Then how did he get there? The answer was found in Samuel's statement years earlier: "For rebellion is as the sin of divination, and presumption is as iniquity and idolatry (15:23)." When Saul heard those words from Samuel, I

Rebellion is as the sin of divination, and presumption is as iniquity and idolatry.

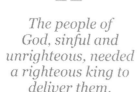

> *The people of God, sinful and unrighteous, needed a righteous king to deliver them.*

am sure he thought the comparison ludicrous. But his rebellious heart led him down this path to a point he could never have imagined. When I was a small boy, my dad would tell us this jungle story about a little boy who adopted a baby leopard. Though he loved it, he was warned not to keep it. I have never forgotten the warning, "Little leopards become big leopards, and big leopards kill." Little sins are no safer than little leopards. The challenge is that little leopards grow slowly, and we lose the ability to see the changes. They are slow and deceptive, just like our sin.

Saul's disgrace is a loud warning about sin, but this passage is not without hope. It is set within a larger context. In this passage, Samuel reminded Saul that his trouble was the result of his sin in dealing with the Amalekites. This account is bracketed by David's victory over the Amalekites (ch. 27, 30). David was the king who obeyed. David did was Saul could not do. It reinforces the truth we have seen throughout: the Lord brings victory to his people by the hand of his righteous anointed. This story begins and ends with David as a reminder that the people of God, sinful and unrighteous, needed a righteous king to deliver them. His example points to a future King—a righteous King who is able to do for us what we cannot do for ourselves. Because of our sinful failure, we too need deliverance, and our hope must be in one who is righteous.

Food for Thought Sin always distorts a person's picture of God. It is sin which causes us to say, "God does not know best. God does not have my good in mind. God does not want me to be happy." It is sin which suggests, "God will forsake you. God cannot forgive you. God does not love you." The serpent distorted the truth about God when he tempted Eve in the Garden. It worked then, and it works now. Sin lies to you about the character of God.

Faith in Action

Think for a moment about the worst sin you ever committed. Did you jump right in or was it a process? All sin looks for is the tiniest opening. It begins small and grows. And like the waistline, it is tough to notice the daily changes. You need to develop a "Zero-tolerance policy" for sin. Make a commitment to fight it immediately. There is no such thing as a little sin.

Prayer

If God has exposed sin in your life, do not ignore it. Do not hide it and do not despair because of it. Jesus is your righteousness. Confess your sin. Turn from it. He has paid sin's debt. He has broken sin's hold. You no longer stand guilty. Exposed sin, though painful, is a blessing. Never forget that there is more mercy in Christ than sin in you. Confess your sin right now and praise God for his forgiveness.

The King We Need

1 Samuel 29–30

When my oldest son Jack was eight, he attended a book club at the library. Before the kids left the library, they were given an assignment to draft their own version of the Bill of Rights. I asked Jack what his would say. He replied, "It will say, 'Everyone do what you want to do.'" So I asked him, "What if your Mom and I want to take both cars and all of our money down to Myrtle Beach for a few months, leaving you and your brothers to take care of yourself at home?" He thought for a moment, "My Bill of Rights will say, 'Everyone do what you want to do, but Jack is King.'" Though not the best solution, he realized the need for leadership. We need someone in charge. We need a king, a leader, a ruler to guide us. What should that leader should look like?

The book of 1 Samuel records Israel's search for a leader. The people wanted a king. They wanted a leader, but they chose poorly. They wanted a king like the other nations; a king to lead them to great victory in battle (8:19–20). They got what they wanted, and their king, Saul, was like the foreign kings. He did win some great

> *Sometimes God has to tell us "no" to accomplish his will.*

battles for them. Yet, it came with a great cost. Saul was the king they wanted, but he was not the king they needed. What kind of king did they need? Chapters 29–30 answer that question. These chapters uncover five different characteristics of David that serve as a template for the right kind of king.

The first characteristic of David was that he was a righteous king. Because of Saul's zeal to murder him, David had been in exile with the Philistines for a year and a half when the Philistines assembled to make war with Israel. As the Philistine forces lined up, the commanders of the Philistine army saw David and a company of Jewish soldiers join the ranks and they did not like it (vv. 1—3). Achish defended David's presence and called him the servant of Saul. He meant to say David was Saul's servant, but what he said by accident was actually the truth. David was Saul's servant. Though Saul had repeatedly attempted to kill David, Saul was God's anointed, and David would not ignore the authority God had set up. Achish also publicly declared that he had found no fault in David. A Philistine king defended David's righteousness. But the commanders of the army did not want David and his men with them (vv. 4—5). They understood the danger of having David, the giant-killer, in their company. Their comment about David presenting "the heads of our men" to Saul revealed their memory of what David did to Goliath years earlier.

Again, Achish affirmed David's righteousness (v. 6). He had found nothing wrong in David. David begged him for an opportunity to fight against the enemies of "my lord the king (v. 8)." This was the fourth time he used that phrase in the book. The first three times (24:8; 26:17, 19) all refer to Saul, and it does here as well. David's intention was to go into the battle and fight for Saul, his lord and king, against the Philistines. A third time, Achish declared the righteousness of David (v. 9). Yet, he still chose to send him away from the battle (vv. 10–11). Why did God not want David to be included in this battle? David's involvement would have brought victory for Israel, but God wanted Israel defeated. Plus, Saul was going to die in battle, and God did not want David anywhere near Saul's death. He wanted David to be utterly blameless in the death of Saul. Sometimes God has to tell us "no" to accomplish his will.

David was not only a righteous king, but he was also a rejected king. David had been running from Saul for the previous ten years. He had just been rejected by the Philistine army. His plan to help Saul in the battle had failed, and he returned home to discover that his wives had been kidnapped, his belongings had been stolen, and his city had been burned (30:1—4). Could it get any worse? Yes. Even those closest to him turned on him (v. 6). Everyone who was in distress, in debt, and in desperation had come to him (22:2). He had taken this riff-raff and cared for them. He had provided for them and led them to great victories. Still they turned on him and rejected him.

In the face of being rejected, David demonstrated that he was a wise king. Wisdom is submission to God as king. Wisdom is the humble recognition that God reigns as sovereign and a humble commitment to follow his will. David showed great wisdom (vv. 6—8). He was in a desperate situation, but he did not rely on his own cunning or ingenuity. He turned to God

Wisdom is submission to God as king.

> *Wisdom is the humble recognition that God reigns as sovereign and a humble commitment to follow his will.*

for strength. He asked God for direction. This was the kind of king the people needed. They needed a king who found his wisdom in the will and direction of God.

Because David wisely submitted to God's direction, he became a victorious king. David and his men found a servant left behind by the army that raided David's city. After giving him food and drink and promising to protect him, they followed him to where the enemy was camped. They attacked the enemy, completely defeated them, rescued every single captive, and restored every possession (vv. 16—20). David did all of this against a much larger army.

After his great victory, David proved to be a gracious king. As he returned, he picked up two hundred of his men who were too exhausted to go into battle (v. 21), and he shared the spoils of battle with them. Some worthless men with David were angry that he shared the spoil with the soldiers who stayed behind. Notice David's perspective: "God gave us the spoil. He preserved us and gave the enemy into our hand. God gave us all of this, what right do we have to withhold it (v. 23)?" David extended grace to the least deserving. He showed grace to the wandering slave. He showed grace to the men who stayed behind. He showed grace to the men who complained. And he showed grace to those who helped him and his men earlier (v. 26).

> *Obeying God's will does not mean understanding why. It means humbly and joyfully submitting to God.*

A generation earlier, when the people cried out for a king, the prophet Samuel warned them that the kind of king they wanted would be a taker (8:13—17), but the kind of king they needed would be a giver. He would rule by grace, not tyranny. David was not the kind of king they wanted, but he was exactly the king they needed.

Food for Thought Sometimes following the will of God is tough. David was certainly frustrated with his inability to participate in the battle. When he heard the news of Israel's defeat, it grieved him. Yet, God was doing far more than David could understand. Obeying God's will does not mean understanding why. It means humbly and joyfully submitting to God, recognizing that even if God revealed why, we might not understand. His plans are far greater and more intricate than our simple minds can comprehend.

Faith in Action

Grace is not fairness. Fairness is getting what we deserve. We do not want what we deserve; we want what we do not deserve. We do not deserve God's kindness, his favor, his protection, or his compassion. Even still God has given us all these things in Christ. Everything good we have is because of grace. Make a list of things God has given you that you do not deserve.

Prayer

Take the list of God's gifts to you and thank him for each and every gift. After you thank him for each gift, ask him for wisdom with how to use these gifts to point others to him.

Conclusion to 1 Samuel

In David, we see the kind of king that Israel needed. They needed a righteous, rejected, wise, victorious, and gracious king. We are not Israelites, and David is not alive now. What difference does this make to us today?

We need to back up before David. In fact, we need to back up all the way to the beginning. After mankind was created, the first man and woman sinned. The curse of their sin was spiritual death (separation from God) and physical death (separation from the body). In that moment when God delivered their punishment, he also made a promise. He promised he would send a Savior to reverse the tragic effects of the curse. The book of Genesis traces this promise from Adam to Abraham. Then, it traces it through Abraham's family, which became the nation of Israel. The book ends by adding a very significant piece to the puzzle. This Savior would be a king (Gen 49:10). A child from the nation of Israel, particularly from the tribe of Judah, would become king and reign until all nations bowed to him in obedience.

For hundreds and hundreds of years following the prophecy in Genesis, Israel did not have a king. But the book of 1 Samuel opens with a prayer, and the prayer ends by saying, "The LORD will judge the ends of the earth; he will give strength to his king and exalt the power of his anointed (2:10)." Who is God's anointed king? It was not Saul. Could it be David? No. Because later God makes a promise to David that one of his offspring will be king forever (2 Sam 7:12–13). David was not the ultimate king—the one who will save us from our sin, bring all nations into obedience, and establish an eternal kingdom. He would come from David's line, however, and he would be like David. In the best characteristics of David, we see a shadow of this future king. From David's life we get a glimpse, impartial and imperfect, but a glimpse of what this future king will be like.

The prophets that followed David incorporated David's qualities into their descriptions of the future king. They looked at David, and said, "The Ultimate King will be a super David. He will be a perfect, eternal David-like King." For instance, listen to Isaiah's description, and how it echoes what we've seen in David's life:

> There shall come forth a shoot from the stump of Jesse, and a branch from his roots shall bear fruit. And the Spirit of the LORD shall rest upon him, the Spirit of wisdom and understanding, the Spirit of counsel and might, the Spirit of knowledge and the fear of the LORD. And his delight shall be in the fear of the LORD. He shall not judge by what his eyes see, or decide disputes by what his ears hear, but with righteousness he shall judge the poor, and decide with equity for the meek of the earth; and he shall strike the earth with the rod of his mouth, and

with the breath of his lips he shall kill the wicked. Righteousness shall be the belt of his waist, and faithfulness the belt of his loins (11:1–5).

Do you notice the same characteristics in the coming King that we have witnessed in David's life? Righteousness, wisdom, strength, and graciousness. He cares for the needy. He rules in justice. He follows the will of God. He defeats the wicked and reigns in glorious strength. But there is another similarity with David. The King would be rejected. Just like David's righteousness was merely a shadow of the future king's righteousness, so too was David's rejection a shadow of the rejection the future king would face (Isaiah 53).

The life of David reveals in shadow the dazzling brilliance of the future king. Take David's righteousness, magnify it a million times, and it still falls short. Take his wisdom, strength, and graciousness, and they reveal just a glimpse of this coming king. Take the pain, suffering, and humility of his rejection, and you get the slightest taste of what the future king would experience to bring salvation to his people. All of which leads us to this question: Has there ever been a king who was perfectly righteous, unquestionably wise, completely victorious, and unfailingly gracious? Has there ever been a king with all of these characteristics, and yet utterly rejected? If there was a king like this, would you follow Him?

Three times, Achish, the pagan king, proclaimed David's righteousness. One of the times, he said, "I find no fault in Him." Jesus Christ, stood before a pagan king named Pontius Pilate, and three times, Pilate declared: "I find no guilt in this man" (Lk 23:4). In a time of great suffering and rejection, David was strengthened by God as he submitted himself and his plans to God's will. On the night before his crucifixion, Jesus was alone in a Garden and submitted his will to the will of his father (Mt 26:39).

David not only faced the rejection of the Philistines, but he also faced the rejection of his own people. The people he had cared for were about to stone him. Jesus was also rejected by all men. The religious leaders of Israel called for his death. One of his own disciples betrayed him. Another denied him. In spite of the rejection, David led his people to great victory, thoroughly defeating the enemies of God. Jesus suffered the rejection of man and God, but because of his sinless life and sacrificial death, he defeated death for all who follow Him (1 Cor 15:54—57). Whether it was a foreign slave, a grumbling soldier, or a weary warrior, David demonstrated grace. He did not give them what they deserved. He gave them grace—what they did not deserve. Jesus embodies grace. He takes the sinner, the slave, the weak, and the wounded, and he makes them his very own (Eph 2:4—7).

Some of my favorite stories share a similar theme. They begin with a people enslaved by a cruel dictator, and they anticipate the return of a good king to deliver them. It could be Aragorn, the king with healing in his hands. Or Aslan, the mighty, righteous lion. Either way, the people's hope is in the coming king. These stories are faint echoes of the grand story of our world. We need a king. Not a king like the kings of this age, but a different kind of king—a special king. We need a righteous, wise, gracious, victorious king. We need a king that was rejected so that we could be accepted. Do you see that this king has come?

Do you follow this king? Jesus Christ died in your place so you could live in glad submission to him. Turn from your rebellion and submit to him alone. He will free you from the chains of sin and pardon you from the penalty of sin.

Conclusion to 1 Samuel

Our world is looking for a Messiah. Each election brings hope in a new ruler—but it is always a false hope. The greatest human kings are a faint imitation of the eternal one. Look around at the wars and genocide, government shutdowns and budget deficits. Is this where you find your hope? We have a greater hope—a hope which will survive when the nations of this world crumble. Our king will return. He will establish an eternal kingdom of mercy and justice. This is our future. Life in his kingdom is the final chapter in the grand story of our world.

Finding L.I.F.E. in Jesus!

Everyone wants to be happy. The hard part is determining exactly what that means. For some, happiness is defined through relationships. They believe that popularity, a huge following on social media, and a significant other produces happiness. For others, happiness is defined through success. They believe that personal achievement, a huge number in their bank account, and plenty of expensive toys produces happiness. For still others, happiness is defined through community. They believe that personal growth, a huge impact for societal change, and embracing diversity produces happiness. And these things do—until they don't.

Experiencing happiness is as difficult as catching the greased pig at the county fair. It appears to be right in front of us, but then it slips through our fingers and is gone. Friends, achievement, and personal growth have the potential to bring happiness into our lives, but when our friends disappear, success eludes us, and we realize that we're incapable of self–transformation, happiness is quickly replaced by disillusionment and depression. The problem with pursuing happiness is that it is an emotion that is driven by our circumstances. And let's be honest—we all tend to have more negative than positive experiences in our lives.

So, what's the answer? Should we keep doing the same things while expecting different results, or should we consider what Jesus has to say about finding our purpose for life? If you want to stay on the hamster wheel while you try to catch up to happiness, you can stop reading here. But if you're ready to consider what God wants to do in your life, please read on.

God never promises happiness in the Bible. Are you surprised to hear that? Instead, he promises something much greater—joy. While happiness is an emotion fueled by circumstance, joy is an attitude fueled by God's Spirit. Happiness is self–determined. In other words, I am the sole determiner of whether I'm happy at any given moment. Joy, on the other hand, is God–determined. God has promised to give us joy, and it isn't based on our circumstances—it's based on God's character and promises.

This is why Jesus never talks about giving people happiness. He knew all too well that chasing happiness is like chasing your shadow. You can never catch it. Instead, he talks about giving people life. He said, "I came that they may have life and have it abundantly (Jn 10:10)." Here, Jesus reveals that the thing people really want, whether they know it or not, is abundant life. To have an abundant life means that you are personally satisfied in all areas of your life, and you experience peace and contentment as a result. Jesus' statement also means that we do not have the capacity to create that kind of life for ourselves. Jesus came in order to give it to us. But how? The Bible tells us that achieving this kind of satisfied life requires us to know something about God, ourselves, and the reason for the death and resurrection of Jesus Christ.

First, we must understand God's **love**. The Bible says that God is love (I Jn 4:8), and God created us so that we could know him and experience his love (Gen 1:26–31). God created us to be worshipers and to live forever in the reality of his glory. And, when sin marred his perfect creation, he created a plan to free men and women from its curse. At just the right time in history, God sent his own Son, Jesus, into our world. "For God so loved the world, that he gave his only Son, that whoever believes in him should not perish but have eternal life (Jn 3:16)." It is God's love that motivates him to restore relationship with those who are separated from him by sin.

Second, we must understand our **isolation**. To be isolated is to be separated from someone, and as a result, to be alone. This is what sin has done to us. It has separated us from the very one we were created to know, love, and worship—God. When Adam and Eve rebelled against God by breaking the lone command he had given them, the entire world was brought under the curse of sin (Gen 3). As a result, God removed them from the Garden of Eden, and their perfect fellowship with God was broken. In an instant, they had become isolated from God because of their sin. From that moment to this, every person born into this world is guilty of sin. The Bible says, "For all have sinned and fall short of the glory of God (Rom 3:23)." Because of this "there is none righteous, no, not one (Rom 3:10)." Further, "The wages of sin is death (Rom 6:23a)." We were created to love and worship God in perfect community, but now because of sin we are isolated from him. Meanwhile, we try to satisfy this desire to know God by pursuing our own happiness, even though we can never hope to attain it. And in doing so, we risk being isolated from God for all eternity.

Third, we must understand our need for **forgiveness.** There is only one way to experience God's love and escape the isolation caused by sin—we must experience God's forgiveness. In spite of sin, God never stopped loving the people he created. He promised Adam and Eve that he would send someone who could fix the problem they had created. When it was time, God sent his own Son, Jesus, to be the world's Savior. This, too, was an act of God's love. The Bible says, "God shows his love for us in that while we were still sinners, Christ died for us (Rom 5:8)." When Jesus died on the cross, he was paying the penalty for our sins (Rom 3:23–26). When God raised Jesus from the dead, it was to demonstrate that forgiveness was available to all who would receive it by faith. Paul explained how this happens in his letter to the Ephesians. "For by grace you have been saved through faith. And this is not your own doing; it is the gift of God, not a result of works, so that no one may boast (Eph 2:8–9)."

The reality is that we cannot experience salvation as a result of our own efforts. We can try to be a good person, go to a church, even give a ton of money to worthy causes— none of these "works" can provide forgiveness. No matter how hard we try, we will always "fall short of the glory of God." That is why we must receive God's offer of forgiveness and salvation by faith. Faith simply means to trust or believe. Salvation requires us to believe that God loves us, that we are isolated from him by our sins, and that his Son Jesus died and was raised to life again to pay the sin debt that we owe God because of our sins. When we take God up on his offer of the gift of salvation, he doesn't just give us forgiveness—he gives us life! The Bible says, "The free gift of God is eternal life in Christ Jesus our Lord (Rom 6:23)."

Fourth, we must understand the **enjoyment** that comes from knowing, loving, and worshiping God. Whether we know it or not, we are slaves to sin until God sets us free (Rom 6:20–23). This was the ultimate reason that God sent his Son, Jesus, to die on the cross for our sins—God sent Jesus so that we could be set free from our sins. Jesus said, "You will know the truth, and the truth will set you free. . . . Everyone who commits sin is a slave to sin. . . . So, if the Son sets you free, you will be free indeed (Jn 8:32–36)." Jesus was teaching us that we must be set free from sin in order to enjoy the life that God has given us—both now and in eternity future. We are set free when we commit our lives to Jesus Christ through faith in his death and resurrection. Then, and only then, will we find joy in the abundant life of Jesus Christ!

So, the question for you is a simple one: Are you ready to experience freedom from sin and the abundant life that Jesus promised you? If so, God is waiting for to talk with him about it (Jer 29:13). Stop right where you are and make this your prayer to God,

> "Father in heaven, I know that I'm a sinner. I know that I've done lots of things that displease you and disappoint you. And, I know that I'm isolated from you because of my sin. I know that if I die without knowing you, I will spend forever separated from you in hell. But, I believe that Jesus is your sinless Son, and I believe that he died on the cross for me. I believe that he died to provide a perfect payment for my sin debt. I believe that you raised him from the dead so that I could experience forgiveness for my sins. Right now, Father, I'm asking you to forgive me of my sins and save me. I am receiving your Son Jesus as my personal Lord and Savior. I will follow you the rest of my life. Please give me the joy

of a life spent knowing, loving, and worshiping you. I ask these things in Jesus' name, Amen."

If you made the decision to accept Jesus as your Savior today, we want to talk with you! Please contact the people at www.seed–publishing–group.com. We would love to talk with you about your decision and help you with your first steps in following Jesus!

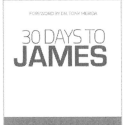

52521109R00128

Made in the USA
Columbia, SC
04 March 2019